CONTENTS

8

16

24

34

40

48

58

66

74

82

CONTENTS

90

98

106

114

122

130

140

146

152

FOREWORD

When Homebuilding & Renovating magazine was launched back in 1990 (it was known as Individual Homes back then), houses built in what has come to be known as 'contemporary style', incorporating modern design ideas, were few and far between. Only architects willing to experiment with their own (or their parents') money and those few self-builders wealthy enough not to have to pay much regard to the conservative tastes of the resale market seemed prepared to break with convention, and build something that incorporated a more innovative room layout or building form.

These early pioneers often had to endure a difficult and sometimes costly journey, through a planning system which, due to its democratic nature, favours mediocrity and is hindered by an inefficient construction industry entrenched in tradition.

In the intervening years, however, a great deal has changed. Prototypes for contemporary detailing have evolved into tried and tested design solutions for most situations. Specialist suppliers and manufacturers have perfected new materials, components and systems that make previously difficult or expensive design concepts more practical, affordable and durable.

Planners, too have become far more open minded towards modern design ideas, as early trailblazers set planning precedents, often after appeal, that have smoothed the way for those who have followed since.

Most importantly, however, contemporary style living has become fashionable and increasingly sought after. People want homes that reflect and respond to the less formal way they now live and the free flowing room layouts that are an integral aspect of contemporary style homes provide just that.

Whilst by no means all self-builders are creating radical contemporary structures like some of the homes featured in this book, the number of exciting and innovative new houses being built in the UK is growing inexorably. Even amongst the less bold, it is fair to say that the majority of self-builders are now choosing to incorporate at least some of the influences of contemporary design, either in the layout of their home or, at very least, in the style of their interiors. Visit any major DIY or furnishing store and it is clear that what was once an exclusive look that required expensive bespoke materials, fixtures, fittings and furniture, is now available to all.

Michael Holmes
Editor, Homebuilding & Renovating Magazine

The homes featured in this book appeared originally in Homebuilding & Renovating Magazine, Britain's best selling monthly title for self-builders and renovators (www.homebuilding.co.uk). The build costs range from an astonishing £60,000 to over £1 million. Each of the projects featured includes floorplans, any available cost details and contacts as well as detailed interviews with the self-builders. If you are interested in having a contemporary home designed and built to your own specifications then this book is definitely for you. There is also a series of eight features looking at design details for contemporary homes, from front doors and staircases, to glass flooring.

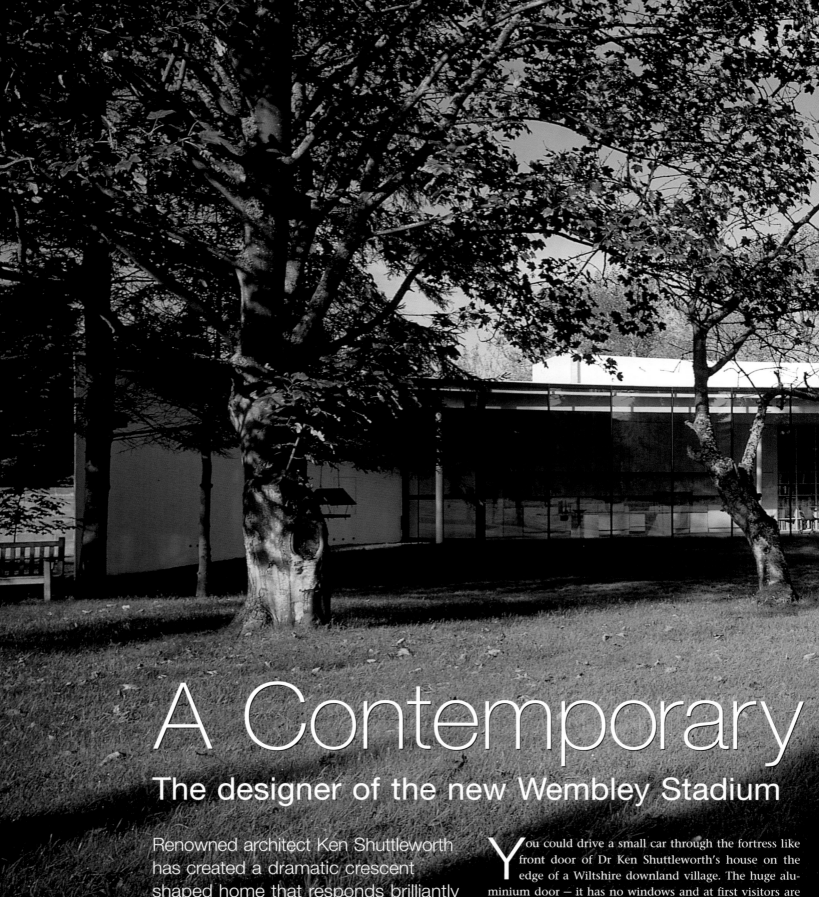

A Contemporary
The designer of the new Wembley Stadium

Renowned architect Ken Shuttleworth has created a dramatic crescent shaped home that responds brilliantly to the conditions of its site, making the most of the views and available sunlight.

Words: **Clive Fewins**   Photography: **Philip Bier**

You could drive a small car through the fortress like front door of Dr Ken Shuttleworth's house on the edge of a Wiltshire downland village. The huge aluminium door – it has no windows and at first visitors are not even sure it is the main entrance to the building – is not the only surprise in the house.

Dr Shuttleworth is a partner in the London architectural practice headed by Lord Foster, and designer of Hong Kong Airport and the new Wembley Stadium. He is a man well versed in the use of glass, steel, concrete and alu-

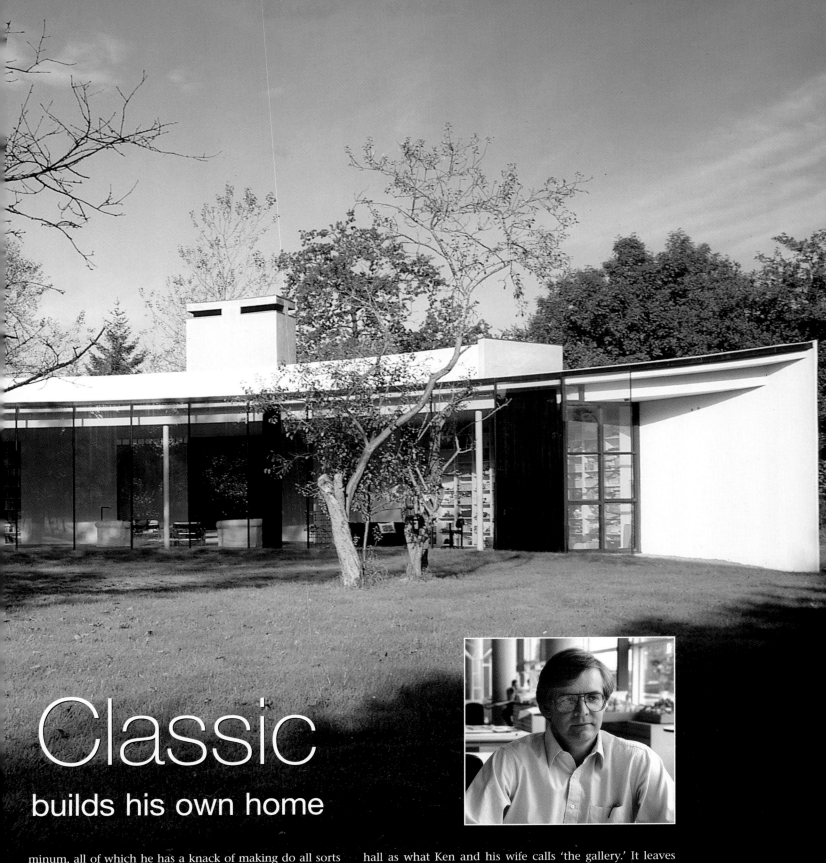

Classic

builds his own home

minum, all of which he has a knack of making do all sorts of things other people might never think of. All four are used in profusion in his own 400m² house, which has won a clutch of awards including a Concrete Society Millennium Award and RIBA Award 2000, since the architect, his wife Seana and their two children moved in three years ago.

As if walking through the front door — once you have found it — of Crescent House is not so much a surprise, the space you then enter is not so much a conventional

hall as what Ken and his wife calls 'the gallery.' It leaves you aghast as you enter because of the height — it rises 5.4m — and the width reduces as you proceed.

The walls of the gallery, built like the rest of the house in cast concrete and plastered on the inside, are lined with paintings — some of them by the Shuttleworths' two young children — and the whole is surmounted by an 'upper gallery' — a small, narrow mezzanine running along the rear wall and accessed by two sets of samba stairs. These are stairs with split treads, allowing them to rise ▶

"Although the curve is structurally significant, the glass wall does not support the flat concrete roof on that side..."

much steeper than a normal staircase and designed as a space saving device.

Halfway along the hall is a giant, 'brutalist' concrete fireplace set into the rear wall. It faces the vast horizontal space of the garden room, where the family cooks, eats, and relaxes and where Jo, 10, and Jaime, 6, play. It is at this stage that you realise the hall, which is lit by means of a high, 30m long, curved clerestory window in jointed glass, cast to form channels which interlock to form a cavity, is the key element that links the two crescent shaped wings.

The couple chose to build their home in Wiltshire because they had owned a house there since the late 80s and were very fond of the area. After a three year search they found a five bedroom, box like house dating from around 1925 on a five acre plot on the outskirts of a village they knew.

"It was built of single skin blockwork and had virtually no insulation. We knew we should knock it down and rebuild eventually but it was big enough for us to live in

for 20 years if necessary," says Ken. They paid £180,000.

The family moved in 1994 and lived there for three years. Then they found – 'by luck', Ken claims – that together with a mortgage of £175,000 from Barclays, they could raise the £345,000 needed to build the sort of house they had decided upon.

"We were very apprehensive about approaching our neighbours – they had sold us the house and land and built a smaller property in which they were living on the adjoining plot," says Ken. "Fortunately when I showed them a model I had made, they quite understood what we wanted to do. We also found the planners very supportive.

They seemed to like the idea of the curved exterior and the way the building fitted into the site, which borders a large area of outstanding natural beauty. They thought the sort of house we planned would improve the area and did not seem to mind the fact that at 400m^2, it was nearly double the size of the previous house. This was because the previous building had a number of outbuildings and workshops that spread over a considerable area."

Ken enlisted colleagues at Ove Arup and Partners to assist with the structural engineering because he knew that the complex design (geometry is his passion) of the flat-roofed structure required some careful engineering.

▲ The south east facing curtain wall is 34m of toughened glass on two layers, from MAG Hansen on 0113 255111.

►

"The main thing was that we intended to use a large amount of glass in the house" he says. "The entire 34m, south east facing curtain wall is glass. It comprises two layers — the outer 15mm layer of toughened glass and the inner 10.5mm laminated glass. There is a 16mm cavity with a Low-E coating on the inside of the outer skin. The whole structure was specially made for us. The way it is anchored into the ground is very complex. At £45,000 it was by far the single most expensive component.

"We wanted one main living space — a garden room — that would allow all the day to day activities of cooking, eating relaxing and playing," says Seana. "There are no divisions in the room, which is bathed in natural light and gives generous views of the garden all the year round."

"I don't think building your own home is the sort of thing you should do too young… I think about 45 is the minimum."

The keys to the whole structure are the two massive concrete 'shear walls' above the front and rear doors and the massive concrete chimney, which rises above the building. The chimney is both practical and the basis of a feature that was very important in the design specification — it houses a massive fireplace. "There is nothing like a log fire. It forms the whole focus of the living area in winter," says Ken, who clears the massive grate of ash once a year.

▼ In addition to the massive fireplace in the 'gallery' there is a warm water trench heating system fired by bulk bottled gas.

"This is an extremely windy site. Despite the fact that we are not high here there is nothing between us and the Bristol Channel. We have planted 1,000 deciduous trees which will eventually reduce the effect of the winds but in the meantime we need great strength in the building to resist this. ▶

"The whole concept was entirely site specific. It was not as though I said to myself, 'I am going to build a house like this whatever the site. The most attractive outlook is on the south east, where we face open country leading across to the Wiltshire Downs. It was to make the most of this that we decided on a semi-circular house, which essentially turned its long back on what we wanted to block out and concentrated its gaze through the glazed wall onto the best views and over the garden."

"The orientation actually helps to prevent overheating in the summer and if it does get too hot we simply swing open the two large glass doors at either end of the south east crescent," Ken explains. The other advantage is that as the sun moves round and hits the solid and translucent walls, the very heavy structure acts as a heat store.

The five bedrooms — all situated within the north west crescent — are windowless apart from narrow skylights against the rear wall. The main source of light is a continuous glazed strip that brings light in from above. "You can lie in bed and focus on the sky and stars," Ken says. "These private spaces, being small and low, give a strong sense of intimacy, security and protection."

"We believe we have succeeded in the brief we set ourselves — to create a house that is environmentally friendly… but functional"

The bedrooms are all irregular shapes, with variants of a crescent in them. The washbasins are all cast in concrete. Except for the vast bulk of the cast concrete chimney and the shear walls, the interior surfaces are all white, intended to reflect the whitewashed walls of traditional Wiltshire buildings. The colour comes from the furnishings and

Fact File costs as of Feb 2001

NAME:	Ken and Seana Shuttleworth
PROFESSIONS:	Architect and artist
AREA:	Rural Wiltshire
HOUSE TYPE:	Single storey, flat roofed
HOUSE SIZE:	400m²
BUILD ROUTE:	Main contractor
CONSTRUCTION:	Solid concrete walls and masonry externally insulated
WARRANTY:	NHBC
SAP RATING:	85
FINANCE:	Private
BUILD TIME:	Jun '96–Mar '97
LAND COST:	£180,000
BUILD COST:	£345,000

TOTAL COST: £525,000

HOUSE VALUE: £1.3m

COST/M²: £862

60% COST SAVING

Cost Breakdown:

Preliminaries	£64,300
Demolition of old house	£1,900
Substructure	£33,400
Frame and roof	£63,600
External walls	£88,200
Windows and external doors	£8,800
Internal walls and partitions	£5,500
Wall floor and ceiling finishes	£12,300
All services	£53,500
Sundries	£13,500
TOTAL	**£345,000**

objects within. The Shuttleworths change towels, cushions, bed linen and other items four times a year to reflect the changing seasons — blue for winter, yellow for spring, green for summer and red for autumn.

"The house was originally going to be a retirement project but we managed to bring it forward," says Ken. "However, I don't think building your own house is the sort of thing you should do too young. I think about 45 is the minimum age. I am 47 now.

"We believe we have succeeded in the brief we set ourselves — to create a house that is environmentally friendly and low maintenance which is not lavish, profligate or precious but calm and functional. Considering the house is currently valued at around £1.3m, I do not consider the building price of £345,000 bad value." ■

USEFUL CONTACTS: **Architect** - Ken Shuttleworth: 020 7794 4574; **Structural Engineers** - Ove Arup and Partners: 020 7636 1531; **Main Contractors** - Dove Brothers: 01375 392391; **Roof Membrane** - Fenland: 01223 840772; **Glass curtain wall** - MAG Hansen: 0113 255 111; **Clerestory Glazing** - Reglit: 0141 613 1414; **Fireplace** - A W Knight: 01225 891469; **Services Engineers** - Roger Preston and Partners: 01628 623423; **Quantity Surveyors** - Davis Langdon and Everest: 020 7497 9000; **Heating** - Drake and Scull: 01703 641641; **Metalwork** - Nic Greening: 0860 836487; **Aluminium Doors** - Trapex: 020 7739 5845; **External Insulation** - Sto: 01505 324262; **Main Joinery** - Unit 22: 020 7278 3872; **Lighting** - Erco: 020 7408 0320

"The huge aluminium door has no windows and at first visitors are not even sure it is the main entrance…"

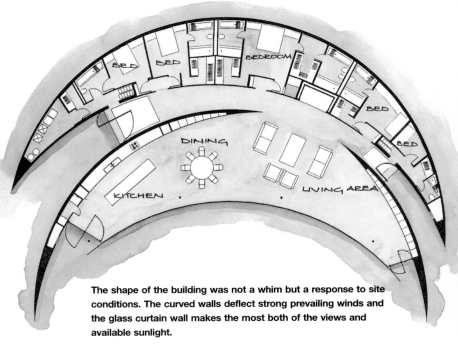

The shape of the building was not a whim but a response to site conditions. The curved walls deflect strong prevailing winds and the glass curtain wall makes the most both of the views and available sunlight.

Off the Wall

The O'Sullivan House has it all, but building this contemporary retreat as a visual extension of the sea wall in Devon stretched both architect and engineer to the limits.

Words: **Debbie Jeffery**
Photography: **Nigel Rigden**

With its copper barrel-vaulted roof, fortress-like stone faced walls apparently growing up out of the water, and projecting timber clad bay complete with an armoured glass floor, Roderic and Sue O'Sullivan's house is architecture with a capital A. Taking the term waterside home to new extremes, its feet literally dabble in the estuary at Salcombe, Devon, and with its ravishingly masculine good looks, taut, clean lines and sharply defined spaces, the breathtaking views and problematic site conditions became the raison d'être for the design. ▶

▼ **The O'Sullivan House nestles subtly between the water's edge and the cliff.**

A radical home in a sensitive waterside location

Almost more grittily interesting than the house, however, is the man who designed it. Stan Bolt, a native Devonian rightly proud of his "working class roots," admits to initially feeling intimidated when training as an architect. His determination fuelled from the age of thirteen by the careless remark of a clueless careers advisor to "be more realistic" in his ambitions, Stan was going to prove his undoubted talents come what may — which he eventually did by winning a RIBA Award for a lavatory and utility room extension, the smallest project ever to win such a prize.

The O'Sullivan family were aware when they purchased this piece of land that building on it would not prove easy. ▶

"The electricians refused to walk on the glass floor and tried stretching over it... but it really is perfectly safe!"

The stunning ▶ **see-through floor in the study area is made of reinforced glass.**

The fireplace ▶ **from Croydon Fireplaces (020 8684 1495) acts as a partition between the two main living areas.**

"We enjoy sailing and had owned a flat in Salcombe for over twenty years," explains Sue, in telling how the family came to build in the area. "We first saw the site from the water whilst out on our boat, and were immediately interested in finding out more."

Formerly a corner of the neighbouring villa's extensive gardens, the site came complete with planning permission and was advertised for sale by auction — with Roderic warned that it would achieve an enormous sum and prove even more expensive to build on. "We gave up and didn't even attend the auction," he recalls. Only later did the family discover that the plot had not

"When we first saw the drawings we were quite shocked — it was not what we had imagined at all..."

reached its reserve price and negotiated privately to purchase the land for a comparatively small (and undisclosed) five figure sum.

Ensuring that both the site and the house were secure and fortified in such an exposed location was of prime importance. Situated at the foot of a steep, almost inaccessible wooded slope overlooking Salcombe Estuary, a planning restriction was imposed requiring all materials and plant to be transported to the site by barge.

"Our architect, Stan Bolt, approached the project extremely methodically, working closely with structural engineer, John Grimes," states Roderic. It was necessary to stabilise and support the coastal slope to prevent slippage and collapse, and the O'Sullivans, who have four children, decided to play safe and attempt to develop the plot in two distinct stages — determining that they could physically and financially build a house only once the necessary preliminary work had been undertaken. This involved clearing the site, rebuilding and repairing the existing sea wall in four hour time slots as the tides allowed, excavating and piling. The coastal slope was cut back to correspond to the 10m contour of the land and stabilised with the construction of a high level concrete retaining wall and an extensive system of rock anchors prior to laying the ground floor slab. Phase one alone was to total £388,000 and took eight months to complete. "I was very keen on a belt and braces approach," remarks Sue. ▶

Fact File costs as of Sept 2001

NAMES: Sue and Roderic O'Sullivan

PROFESSIONS: Teacher and solicitor

AREA: Devon

HOUSE TYPE: Four bedroom detached

HOUSE SIZE: 282m²

BUILD ROUTE: Main contractor

CONSTRUCTION: Loadbearing masonry supporting exposed steel frame

WARRANTY: Architect's certificate

SAP RATING: 100

FINANCE: Private

BUILD TIME: 16 months

LAND COST: Undisclosed

BUILD COST: £808,542

CURRENT VALUE: £1.3m

COST/M²: £2,867

Cost Breakdown:

Phase One
Preliminaries	£206,000
Demolition/site clearance	£3,000
Sea Wall	£51,250
Piling/ground floor slab	£52,250
Rock excavation and high level retaining wall	£43,500
External works/drainage	£32,000
Total	**£388,000**

Phase Two
Preliminaries	£133,989
External Walls	£22,739
Internal Walls	£10,940
Upper floors	£8,633
Staircase	£3,989
Roof	£47,737
Frame	£23,531
External doors/windows	£22,059
Internal doors	£5,212
Balconies and terrace	£13,856
Wall finishes	£15,160
Floor finishes	£16,275
Ceiling finishes	£4,334
Fittings and furniture	£23,807
Mechanical/plumbing and electrical installation	£48,506
Fireplace	£4,772
External works	£11,448
Drainage	£3,485
Total	**£420,542**

TOTAL	**£808,542**

The dining room is dominated by the glorious external views over the estuary.

The hallway is overlooked by a gallery and the double height space and glass ceiling helps to shed light into this potentially dark area.

First Floor

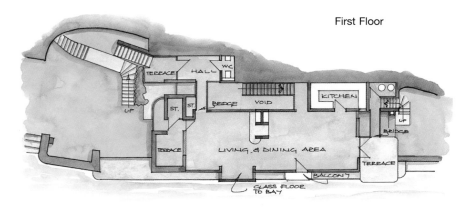

Ground Floor

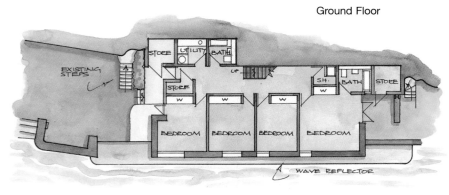

"[Stan Bolt] has given us more from the site than we ever thought could be achieved…"

Useful Contacts

Chartered Architect — Stan Bolt:
01803 852588

Structural Engineer - — John Grimes
Partnership: 01752 690533

Services Engineer — Dodd, Cumming
& Love: 01752 253559

Main Contractor — Dean & Dyball
Construction Ltd: 01392 460500

Steelwork — JCR Engineering:
01803 520232

Walling stone — Lakeview Quarry:
01458 224033

Steel windows — Monk Metal
Windows Ltd: 01213 514411

Glazing — Pilkington UK Ltd:
01744 692000

Flat roofing — Sarnafil Ltd:
01603 748985

Copper roof — W H Joyce & Sons:
01752 668381

External doors — Martin Roberts:
01795 476161

Internal doors — D. W. Archer:
01179 710294

Entrance door — Sharman Joinery:
01271 375481

Timber floors — Junckers Ltd:
01376 517512

Western Red Cedar — D W Archer:
01179 710294

Balau Decking — Morgan & Co:
01634 290909

**Joinery; bathroom, utility room,
window cills & staircases** —
Fitzroy Joinery: 01752 562452

Fireplace — Croydon Fireplaces:
020 8684 1495

Slate flooring — Delabole Slate:
01840 212242

Light fittings —
Concord Lighting Ltd: 01273 515811
Marlin Lighting Ltd: 020 8894 5522

Sanitaryware — West One Bathrooms
Ltd: 020 7720 9333

Kitchen units — Applied Shopfitting
Ltd: 01364 643855

The existing site of the proposed dwelling, at 3.6m above Ordnance Datum (AOD), had experienced flooding as a result of waves breaking over the sea wall. This, coupled with predictions that tide levels may rise by up to 420mm over the next 70 years due to global warming, resulted in rebuilding the sea wall with a wave deflector – calculated by the consulting engineer to combat a potential wave height of up to 1.5m – and raising the ground floor as high as practically possible on the site.

The house is a reverse level affair, with a large open plan living room leading out onto decked terraces and cantilevered balconies and taking full advantage of the views. This first floor was constructed in an altogether different manner to the robust reinforced concrete walls which contain the bedrooms and bathrooms below. The loadbearing masonry of the ground floor supports the first floor exposed steel frame, terminating in the gentle curve of the copper roof.

"We gave Stan a detailed brief of our needs," says Roderic, whose primary residence is a chintzy and traditional London flat which now feels cluttered when compared to the contemporary new house. "This included the need for plenty of bathrooms to accommodate our children, and we now have a really big walk-in shower room, with a large utility area for washing and drying clothes. The design aesthetics were left almost entirely to Stan, however, and when we first saw the drawings we were quite shocked – it was not what we had imagined at all – although we immediately warmed to it. He has given us more from the site than we ever thought could be achieved."

It has to be said that the minimalist style dwelling would not suit an untidy family. Each room is streamlined to within an inch of its life: a row of bedrooms leads off from the lower hallway through grey doors, with all beds made up in pristine white linen to complement the black carpet and grey built-in wardrobes. Light reflecting from the water outside ripples on the ceilings. Bathrooms are identically tiled in white, with slate floors and perfectly folded grey towels. It is almost a shock to stumble upon the single room featuring primary colours, in the form of duvet covers on bunk beds.

Upstairs, the glass floor holds a child-like fascination for most visitors and is highlighted by the fact that this screened workstation bay does not feature forward facing windows. Such a clever conceit provides a degree of privacy and contrasts with the vast expanses of glass on this level, drawing your eye downwards to the lapping waves beneath your feet and, surreally, a bobbing red buoy. Your mind tells you it must be safe to stand on, and yet somehow it takes a superhuman effort to tread here.

"The electricians refused to walk on the glass and tried stretching over it," laughs Stan, forcefully leaping up and down to prove his point, "but it really is perfectly safe!" ∎

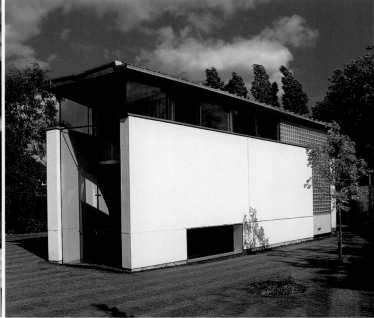

Shining Light

Michael and Lindsay Hird's new home is an extraordinary modern design on a brownfield site in the most ordinary of settings.

Words: **Debbie Jeffery**   Photography: **Nigel Rigden**

Building your own home is all about fantasy. If you want unusual shapes and features – and they are within your budget – then surely you should go for it? Unfortunately cautious planners and practical constraints frequently result in half-hearted architecture. Michael and Lindsay Hird have been fortunate – and brave – enough to persevere with their dream, however, and are now the proud owners of what has been dubbed 'The Glass House'.

The setting of their home is not ideal: cosying up near brick 1930s semis and next door to a petrol filling station in Doncaster, the market town of South Yorkshire, its surroundings simply serve to further highlight the uncompromising design. Inspired by Gio Ponti's Pirelli Building in Milan, the floor plan has a diamond shape with four free-

standing walls rendered with concrete and painted white. These are separated by high windows, with a thin row of windows running along the top, and end walls made of huge glass sheets.

Lindsay's brother, architect Colin Harwood, literally took a section through the Pirelli tower and developed the idea to create a contemporary, open plan layout with clean, angular lines and a light and spacious feel. Interior features include a spectacular glass staircase whilst, beneath the living area, a large basement with underground parking gave rise to a 'Batman's cave' comparison.

"The most difficult part of the project was finding a suitable plot, because you are up against developers and dealing with the planners," says Michael of their suburban brownfield site: half an acre of old council land. With the

An extraordinary new house on a very ordinary plot

plot bordering a Conservation Area, the council (who have congratulated themselves as being 'one of the most progressive local authorities in the country') initially rejected the white concrete finish of the walls, and the build was greatly delayed whilst the Hirds employed a planning consultant to successfully appeal on their behalf. "Compromising by cladding the house in red brick would have been unthinkable," states Michael. "It was such an integral part of the design that there really was no alternative as far as we were concerned."

"Such innovative designs and contemporary materials are usually reserved for the commercial sector."

The neighbours were not so sure — becoming anxious as the lozenge-shaped blockwork structure rose out of the ground that it could be a car-wash, an art gallery or even a crematorium. Certainly such innovative designs and contemporary materials are usually reserved for the commercial sector.

The Hirds had been living in a village 45 minutes drive from Michael's Doncaster business — recycling railway sleepers and tracks. Moving closer to work would mean more time to spend with Lindsay and their two children, and was one of the main reasons behind building their own home. "Colin had designed and converted a chapel for us where we were able to remain whilst our new house was being built," Lindsay explains.

Having already learnt much from the process of converting, the couple were able to bring firm ideas regarding their requirements to the new build project. Space and light were vital considerations, and 'Bennetthorpe House' certainly has plenty of both. Although Lindsay and ▶

With each ▶ pane fitting flush against the other without the need for conventional frames there is absolutely no room for error. Such a system is rarely used for domestic housing. "It's so much easier for builders to whack up brick walls and put in tiny little windows," says Colin.

"Quotes from various builders had been for more than double the original estimated budget…"

▲ The staircase to the basement garage is hidden between stark white walls.

Michael were keen to leave as much of the design to Colin as possible, they envisaged that clashes could occur working so closely with a family member and, inevitably for such a complex venture, a number of problems did arise. Colin's previous work revolved around designing interiors and this was his first ever new build. He preferred an 'organic', fluid approach whilst the builders demanded detailed specifications. The resulting confusion ensured that what was initially hoped would be a 12 week build spread over several months. "I had to write a letter to both Colin and Glen, the building contractor, telling them to calm down!" Michael laughs.

Additionally, Colin had encountered difficulties finding structural engineers to work on the project, whilst quotes from various builders had been for more than double the original estimated budget. A suitable building contractor was eventually found, the council tractor shed which had stood on the site was demolished and construction of the basement and underground garage in concrete blocks got underway. ▶

A huge blockwork and granite fireplace takes pride of place in the sitting room.

The master ▲ bedroom suite enjoys great views thanks to the wall of glazing and large windows on both sides.

Exact measurements were vital for a building of such strange angles and varying levels but, when the 30 purpose-made concrete beams arrived to make up the ground floor, they fitted precisely. "I was slightly worried," admits Colin. "Even though we were using fairly basic construction methods, the odd shapes, thirteen degree angles and the amount of glass for a domestic building made every calculation count."

"It is the use of glass which steals the show: that staircase, Ibstock glazed bricks and the huge panels…"

Even the roof of this house is out of the ordinary: a lightweight aluminium system of double skin insulated construction. This roofing 'sandwich' incorporates an outer 'Kalzip' sheet, mineral fibre insulation, a vapour control layer and liner sheet on structural decking. The insulation depth is accommodated between two skins by selecting from a range of clip heights, with the system proving very permeable — which reduces the build up of moisture and condensation.

With delays occurring at almost every turn the Hirds had no choice but to move into their unfinished home once they had sold the chapel. Michael is philosophical, however, believing that these additional weeks did not dramatically affect the price of the project and, although unwilling to divulge exact build costs, he does warn other self-builders: "You will always be over budget."

Fact File costs as of January 2002

NAME: Michael and Lindsay Hird

PROFESSIONS: Railway contractor

AREA: Doncaster

HOUSE TYPE: Contemporary

HOUSE SIZE: 400m²

BUILD ROUTE: Building contractor and self-managed subcontractors

CONSTRUCTION: Rendered blockwork and glass

WARRANTY: Architect's certificate

SAP RATING: Not known

FINANCE: Private

BUILD TIME: 11 months

All the glass, including the glass staircase — the first one of its kind in the world - came from Austrian company Eckelt Glass, which specialises in high performance glazing and design.

The three ▶ storey house was inspired by the diamond-shaped floor plan of the Pirelli Building in Milan, with basement storage and underground parking, a largely open plan living area on the ground floor and bedrooms on the upper floor.

USEFUL CONTACTS: **Designer** - Colin Harwood: 07940 773212 **Glass Installation** - Dean Wheeler: 07989 305348 **Glazing Manufacture** - Eckelt Glass: 0043 7252 894 255 **Structural Engineer** - Darryl Blackwood: 0161 228 2610 **Structural Steelwork** - A&D Fabrications: 01302 341758 **Stainless Steel and decking** - Tilewind: 01302 721205 **Basement Tanking** - Ruberoid: 01707 822 222 **Underfloor Heating** - Thermoboard: 01392 444122 **Timber Floor Insulation** - Aran Joinery: 01302 330231 **Precast concrete floors & stairs** - Tarmac: 01335 360601 **Roof Insulation** - Profile Roofing: 01709 790326 **Specialist Welding** - Armthorpe Gordon: 01302 830202 **Door knobs etc** - Thews: 0151 709 9438 **Stainless Steel Chimney** - Selkirk: 01271 326633 **Precast concrete block chimney** - Isokern: 01202 861650 **Joinery** - Lee Kendrick: 01302 337514 Mick Rowley: 01302 361140 **Stainless Steel Kitchen** - GEC Anderson: 01442 826999

Now completed, however, the finished house is stunning. Transparent walls give glimpses of the chic interiors, with cherry wood floors and a huge open fire in an otherwise minimalist space. Michael says he would be happy to build again whilst Lindsay isn't quite so sure — she loves her new boat-shaped home and, with five bedrooms, the 400m² property provides more than enough space for the whole family. But it is the use of glass which steals the show: that staircase, Ibstock glazed bricks, and the huge panels of glazing all work together to artfully reflect light and shadow onto the walls and surfaces of this truly amazing home. ■

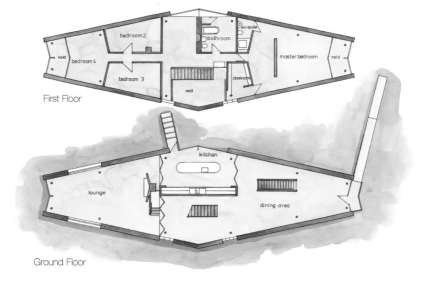

First Floor

Ground Floor

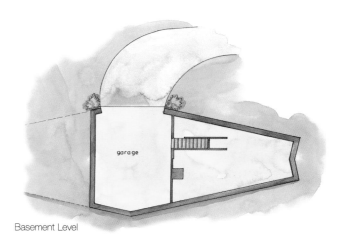

Basement Level

stainless steel

for looks for life

from the stainless steel specialists GEC Anderson

Whatever the building: public or private, commercial or residential. A completely dependable and adaptable range of superb stainless steel products. From sink and worktop options – with a choice of finishes and edge detailing – to cabinets, shelving and sanitaryware.

Impressively high on quality, good looks and performance. Reassuringly low on maintenance.

Standard and made-to-measure versatility for each environment.

Contact us for full details of our product range or visit **www.gecanderson.co.uk**

GEC ANDERSON

GEC Anderson Limited
Oakengrove, Shire Lane
Hastoe, Tring
Hertfordshire HP23 6LY

Tel: +44 (0)1442 82 6999
Fax: +44 (0)1442 82 5999
info@gecanderson.co.uk
www.gecanderson.co.uk

sinks and worktops ■ cabinets and shelving ■ sanitaryware

Perfectly Formed

John and Eleanor Stewart have built a beautiful contemporary style home with a cleverly compact layout that makes excellent use of space.

Words:
Caroline Ednie

Photography:
Andrew Lee

Heading south through the villages towards Aberdeen, a new addition to this relatively flat landscape has stopped more than a few passing motorists in their tracks. With good reason too. For the new home of John and Eleanor Stewart has thrown down the gauntlet in terms of presenting an alternative model to the samey and not very contextually savvy kit houses that currently pepper the Scottish landscape.

In fact the Stewarts' house, designed by Edinburgh based Richard Murphy Architects, is a cracking model of cool yet cosy contemporary design, that not only respects the integrity of the rural setting, but importantly has its feet firmly on the ground in terms of budget. Indeed, for the none too princely sum of £110,000, the Stewarts are now happily ensconced in a beautifully bespoke architectural gem, which just goes to show that it is possible to achieve a leading edge architect designed house without entering financial cloud cuckoo land.

The tern ▶ coated steel roof appears to float over the house.

Eleanor Stewart is, not surprisingly, very proud of her new home and unfazed by all the attention it's been attracting. "I'm hoping that it does generate interest because if you've seen the majority of housing being built locally, you'll appreciate what has been achieved here," she explains.

And what has been achieved is not "cobbling together a kit house to make it look like a typical one and a half storey Highland building," explains architect Richard Murphy. "I totally reject that way forward, it's a horrible aping of the past," he adds. Instead the architects have ▶

"In terms of budget, this is an extraordinarily impressive house for a build cost of just over £100,000…"

▲ On a nice summer's day the whole house can be opened to the garden. In winter occupants can shelter within behind cherry wood shutters that close off all of the windows.

The kitchen ▶ was supplied by Aberdeen-based Denmore Kitchens (01224 826776).

adopted a very site-specific approach. "Our idea for the house was to be long and sleek in the countryside. The landscape is nothing spectacular as far as Scotland goes, so I was interested in making something low, horizontal and floating."

The architects came up with a linear, single storey design on an east-west orientation. The building is constructed by means of a galvanised steel frame and clear-stained timber window frames to the south, with dry-dash blockwork to the north elevation. Load bearing blockwork also features internally. A tern coated steel roof completes the "low, horizontal and floating" picture.

"The major difference between this house and other indigenous buildings is that other Highland houses tend to be dominated by the roof, so although ours is very conscious, it doesn't take the usual form," continues Richard. "Although it is still making a big statement about the whole idea of living under a roof, embracing the idea of shelter. It's a big roof that floats over the building."

The roof overhangs the southern glazed façade primarily to reduce the glare of the direct summer sunlight, yet it

also succeeds in harnessing the lower winter sun in the living area. "The beautiful thing about an architect designed house is that you can influence its orientation. In our case the sun hits our bedroom first thing in the morning, then goes down in the living area downstairs just above the fireplace. It's a beautiful effect. And in terms of solar gain we only need the heating on in the late autumn and winter. It's cosy enough without it," explains Eleanor.

And just in case extra cosiness was required, an all embracing system of insulated cherry wood shutters along the roof lights and glazed south façade means that the whole house can be completely cocooned. As Richard ▶

You first · Lloyds TSB Scotland

Safe hands

By moving day our Lloyds TSB Scotland mortgage had taken care of all the big problems, leaving us plenty of time to take care of all the small ones.

Call **0800 056 0156*** for more information.

YOUR HOME MAY BE REPOSSESSED IF YOU DO NOT KEEP UP REPAYMENTS ON YOUR MORTGAGE.

Lloyds TSB Scotland plc Registered office: Henry Duncan House, 120 George Street, Edinburgh EH2 4LH. Registered in Scotland no. 95237. Lloyds TSB is authorised and regulated by the Financial Services Authority and a signatory to the UK Banking Codes. We are members of the Financial Services Compensation Scheme and the Financial Ombudsman Service. Before agreeing a loan we will want to satisfy ourselves about the suitability of your application. This will include assessing your ability to afford the payments and valuing the property. Applicants must be 18 years or over.
*Lines are open 8am-6pm, Monday to Friday. You can also leave your details on our answerphone outside these times. Calls may be monitored or recorded.

▲ For convenience a doorway between the master en suite bathroom and the family shower room links the two spaces. The door can be locked when they receive visitors.

Murphy explains "the house has three manifestations of its skin. On a nice summer's day you can open the whole house to the garden, then on a normal day the house is collecting solar gain, and finally at night or in the winter you've got all the shutters closed. The whole thing about moveable insulation is that it's empowering the people in the house to make an energy efficient home. You have the insulation when you are in a situation of net heat loss, and you can take the insulation away when you are in a position of net heat gain. That's a very simple idea but very rarely built."

By way of a contrast to the ever changing personality of the south elevation, the north façade is virtually blank, pierced only by entrance doors and tiny windows. And it is along this semi-public side of the house that the architects have, logically, located the internal services and utility areas. These emanate from an impressive connecting corridor which runs parallel with the north façade. The corridor's cherry lined floors, doors and sloping shutters create a warm, introverted feel, while the addition of a shaft of south facing rooflights, with cleverly placed mirrors at the end, creating the illusion that the corridor continues further, imaginatively balances the whole.

The master bedroom with en suite, two family bedrooms and a shower room are located along the internal corridor to the south. Eleanor admits that "although we are very happy with the house, if we had been able to afford it we would have made the bedrooms a wee bit bigger. But they're fine, and as the architects would say 'bedrooms are just for sleeping in.' You've got to have your space in the living areas."

"Although we are very happy with the house, if we had been able to afford it I would have made the bedrooms a wee bit bigger. But you've got to have your space in the living areas."

To prove her point, the open plan, split level living areas are beautifully spacious. At the heart is a simple monochromatic kitchen with polished black granite worktops and white finished cupboards that the couple bought off the shelf according to the architect's instructions. Adjoining is a roomy dining area, overlooking the expansive terrace, where the couple admit that they spend most of their time. Finally, steps lead down to the living room which nestles snugly into the south west slope of the open landscape. A raised hearth features a wood burning stove at its heart, and there are clever touches, such as a two way log bunker beside the stove.

The stove figures primarily as a winter warmer, as most of the warmth is normally achieved by underfloor heating. As John explains, "when the stove – which is at the bottom level of the house – is on, the heat just rises and heats up the entire house. All the rooms are on a thermostat for underfloor heating and when the stove comes on it picks up the air and the thermostats cut back. It's a very efficient system and very cosy."

In fact, so far the Stewarts, who fittingly moved into their 21st century home on Hogmanay 2000, have had no real problems with the new house, which is testament not only to the thoroughness of the design, but also in large part to the efforts of the building contractors. As Eleanor explains, "this is the first time the local contractors had done anything like this. When we initially asked Ian, the contractor, what he thought of the balsa wood model of the house that the architects had produced, he said "Well, it's different." And when we asked him if he thought he could build it, he said 'Aye, I can give it a go!' He's done a good job and I'm proud that he took it on."

In terms of plain sailing, planning also proved to be something of a cinch. The Stewarts admit that the only compromise that had to be reached was in the design of the down pipe. Apart from that they got exactly what they wanted, although it did go 10% over budget, admits Eleanor.

Still, in terms of budget, this is an extraordinarily impressive house for a build cost of just over £100,000. And having just picked up the Best Design Award at The Aberdeenshire Design Award Scheme, and a whole plethora of others, this model of site specific rural architecture also looks like it is gaining the recognition and reputation that it deserves. ∎

USEFUL CONTACTS: **Architect** – Richard Murphy Architects: 0131 220 6125; **Main contractor** – Gardiner Building Management: 01651 842466 **Structural Engineer** – Peter Gallon: 01224 312633; **Sliding Door** – Hillaldum Coburn: 020 8336 1515; **Ironmongery** – Hafele: 01698 422525; **Lighting** – Reggiani: 020 8953 0855; **Steelwork** – WA&S Higgins: 01651 851651; **Kitchen** – Denmore Kitchens: 01224 826776; **UFH** – Invisible Heating: 01854 613161

Fact File costs as of Jan 2003

NAMES: Eleanor and John Stewart
PROFESSIONS: Property Developer
AREA: Aberdeenshire
HOUSE TYPE: 3 bedroom house
HOUSE SIZE: 115m²
BUILD ROUTE: Main contractor + DIY
CONSTRUCTION: Steel frame

WARRANTY: Architect's Certificate
SAP RATING: 97
FINANCE: Standard Life
BUILD TIME: Summer '99 – Dec '00
LAND COST: Undisclosed
BUILD COST: £110,000
HOUSE VALUE: Unknown
COST/m²: £957

The house sits low against the landscape, with a simple dry-dashed render to complement the simplicity of the structure.

Andrew and Paula Watson have created a groundbreaking Modernist style home using the latest insulated formwork construction system.

Words:
Clive Fewins

Photography:
Jeremy Phillips

When they have finally put the finishing touches to their new self-build home in a village near Nottingham, Andrew and Paula Watson are contemplating placing a noticeboard outside on which people can attach their comments. "I am not expecting them all to be polite," says Andrew, a chartered surveyor and developer, whose ambition for as long as he can remember has been to build his own house in a contemporary international style.

He has certainly succeeded. But if previous remarks are anything to go by, the comments on the board are likely to include the phrases "an eyesore," "like a fish factory," (Andrew's sister's comment) and "like an igloo."

The latter remark came from Andrew and Paula's five children and resulted from the main form of construction – the Beco permanent insulated formwork system, in which interlocking lightweight polystyrene blocks act as a mould for the concrete that is poured between them to form the walls and then stays permanently in position afterwards.

Some of the adverse comments originated during the seven-and-a-half month construction phase, when residents of the quiet, genteel lane in which the house is situated found themselves confronted almost daily by giant lorries carrying steel beams and large tankers full of liquid concrete. They also had to contend with several visits from a 50 tonne crane that was used to erect the steel frame and lift the beam and block system supporting the first floor and roof.

The heavy concrete roof and massive steel frame is one area in which Andrew admits that his approach to building the house might have verged on overkill at times. "We could have saved a lot of money by using straightforward blockwork in the walls," he says. However he loves the highly insulated solid walls, and also their thickness. In the two storey section of the building – the kitchen is single storey – the walls are 470 mm thick, with the Beco blocks wrapped round the steel sections that form the frame. The concrete-filled blocks take up all but 32mm of this width, the rest being plasterboard on the inside and a render on the exterior.

As you might imagine, the U-values in the roof, floors and walls are very high, particularly as the south-facing frontage is largely glazed, including a striking glass clerestory running right along the front of the house. This brings light flooding into the full-height atrium, which is supported by nine full height round steel columns. ▶

The amount of ▶ glass in the southern elevation necessitated the use of a structural steel frame.

Building a
Modernist style home

Vision of the Future

"Andrew coped very well with some of the ruder remarks but I am a bit more sensitive than him…"

The kitchen ▶ (ABOVE AND RIGHT) is from CP Hart (0161 214720).

Outside, the fear of overheating is alleviated by a striking array of sun louvres above the ground floor windows at the south-facing front. Inside the plain white, Minimalist atrium, storage cupboards are concealed neatly behind plain white doors stretching right along the front of the house. The single-storey kitchen, breakfast room and playroom leads off it in a T-shape to the south. The house is awash with light from the front but the rear of the lounge, which is the full height of the building, is glazed to bring in additional light which bounces off the plain white walls in all directions. Like the large kitchen, the lounge is doorless.

Andrew and Paula are delighted with the way the house has turned out. "Andrew coped very well with some of the ruder remarks but I am a bit more sensitive than him about such things," says Paula. "But then this is a very quiet lane and the build did cause a lot of disruption. Fortunately our immediate neighbours were very supportive and our planning officer, Norman Jowett, was right behind us from the start. He took a lot of flack himself, although he told us that towards the end of the project he did receive a few complimentary phonecalls. Strangely enough the planning consent went through on delegated powers."

Andrew acted as project manager for the build. Having sold their previous house in a nearby village early in 2000 (their first self-build and home of five years) they lived in temporary accommodation nearby during the build. ▶

A six metre ▶ long gallery bridge, overlooking the living room (BELOW), links the master bedroom and children's rooms (RIGHT).

Andrew moved his office to a temporary building on a corner of the six acre site, which had previously contained a 1960s bungalow. From there he was able to supervise the seven-and-a-half month build at the same time as running his business.

The key builders were some of Andrew's own workforce whom he had known for ten years or so. Nevertheless he admits that some aspects of the technique demanded a steep learning curve. "Beco is marvellous fun to work with but we had quite a few bursts when the concrete broke through the polystyrene," he says.

For this he blames not the Beco system but the way he and his team went about the job. "Some of the bursts were where the Beco blocks had to fit round the posts of the steel frame, which was a bit tricky," he says. "Many of the problems were caused because we were trying to do it too fast. The Beco formwork needed more support on both sides as the blocks were being filled. Also I think we did not control the rate at which we poured the concrete into the blocks as well as we might have done."

There is so much solar heat gain in the house that air conditioning is vital. The Watsons have had to use their gas fired underfloor heating very little. This style of heating is ideally suited to the clean, crisp lines of the house. There is nothing out of place: the furniture, right up to the prototype designer chair, made by Andrew's oldest son, Seng, is carefully chosen.   ▶

"Our only regret sometimes is that our house is not situated in California or Sydney…"

▲ A glazed atrium runs across the front of the house where the structure is supported by nine full height round steel columns.

Useful Contacts

Architect – Allison-Pike Partnership:	01663 763000
Structural engineer – Howard Stanley-Pratt:	0115 953 9993
Builders – Park Portfolio:	01949 829101
Structural formwork – Beco Products:	01652 651641
Air conditioning – Lynx Climate Control:	01522 788721
Horizontal solar shades – Swift welding:	01298 79381
Underfloor heating – Rehau:	0161 777 7400
Roofing membrane – Trocal:	01753 522212
Roofing contractor – Metclad:	01623 720032
Steel windows – DNS windows:	0115 963 6361
Clerestory windows on first floor – Reglit:	0141 613 1414
Glazing – Vision Systems:	01843 825817
External render – Marmorit:	01179 821042
Oak floors – Floorco:	01933 418899
Stone floors – Stone Age:	01179 238180
Marble floor – Fyfe Glenrock:	01224 744101
Kitchen and sanitary fittings – C P Hart:	0161 214 7206
Sliding room dividers – Dividers Modernfold: 01269 844877	

The open fire on the ground floor is a two-way feature shared between the sitting room and the snug. Its steel flue, visible in the main sitting room, makes a strong statement. Another 'industrial' feature, in addition to the steel frame and the full-height atrium is the deep, frameless glass porch, while the roof is covered by a single ply membrane on a tapering bed of insulation – again an adaptation of an industrial system.

Another notable feature is the sliding screen between the two older children's ground floor bedrooms. This is repeated upstairs – again between the two other children's rooms. The object is to make the spaces more versatile when entertaining overnight guests.

From the upstairs children's bedrooms you pass along a six metre long bridge to the master bedroom. Reflecting much of the downstairs, this room has plain white walls and no curtains. There is a cleverly-designed permanent dividing screen situated behind the bed that leads to the dressing room, walk-in wardrobe and shower room and wc.

The main upstairs bathroom is at the other end of the house. It connects with the guest bedroom as well as the

Fact File costs as of Aug 2002

NAMES: Andrew and Paula Watson

PROFESSIONS: Developer & housewife

AREA: Nottinghamshire

HOUSE TYPE: Six bedroomed flat-roofed contemporary-style house

HOUSE SIZE: 423m²

BUILD ROUTE: Main contractor

CONSTRUCTION: Beco Wallform system around steel frame

WARRANTY: Zurich

SAP RATING: 97

FINANCE: Private plus £200,000 mortgage from Lloyds TSB

BUILD TIME: Nov '00 – June '01

LAND COST: £245,000	**7%**
BUILD COST: £500,000	**COST**
TOTAL COST: £745,000	**SAVING**

HOUSE VALUE: £800,000

COST/m²: £1,182

Cost Breakdown:

Substructure	£40,000
Drainage	£5,000
Steel frame	£20,000
Upper floors	£15,000
Exterior walls	£80,000
Roof	£35,000
Stairs	£10,000
Exterior windows and doors	£125,000
Interior windows & partitions	£25,000
Interior doors	£15,000
Finishes	£40,000
Fittings	£30,000
Mechanical and electrical	£40,000
Fees	£12,500
Misc	£7,500
TOTAL	**£500,000**

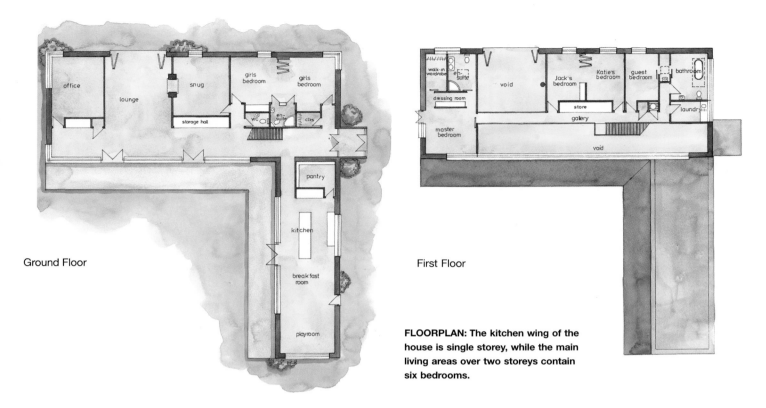

Ground Floor

First Floor

FLOORPLAN: The kitchen wing of the house is single storey, while the main living areas over two storeys contain six bedrooms.

landing. The stunning slab containing the washbasins is cut out of solid marble, so heavy it had to be craned in. It was specially made at a cost of £2,500.

One big expense that Andrew and Paula had not anticipated was the cost of below-ground works, which involved 45 deep piles being built to support the beam and block ground floor slab. This was necessary because of the fears of shrinkage due to the clay subsoil and the large number of yew and redwood trees on site, all of which were sub-ject to tree preservation orders. "Because of this and the £500,000 build cost, in terms of investment we have to take a long term view of the project," says Andrew. "The cost of the plot, which included the previous house but no planning permission, was very high. We did not aim to make an instant profit and although we have not ruled out another self-build, this will be it for a while. Our only regret is that our house is not situated in California or Sydney, where it would look very much at home!" ∎

◀ **The striking white external render is from Marmorit (01179 821042).**

Elegant
Simplicity

Sarah and Stephen Gee have created a new home with beautiful contemporary style living spaces concealed within a simple, economic, steel frame structure.

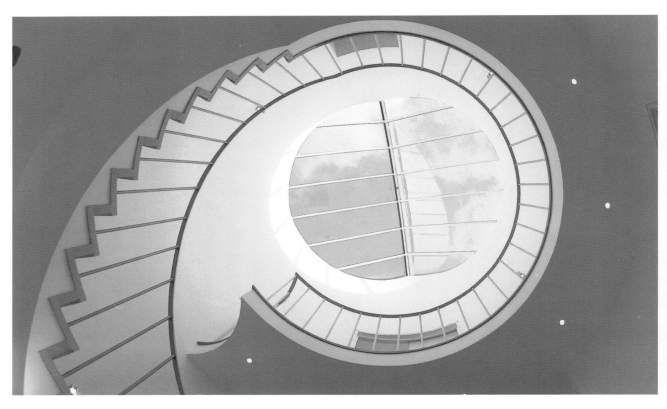

The dramatic circular hallway and curved stone staircase were inspired by a visit to the opera.

Words: **Debbie Jeffery**   Photography: **Leigh Simpson**

"Six years ago we decided to buy a piece of land in Hurstpierpoint, Sussex, where I grew up," explains Sarah Gee. She and her husband, Stephen, were on holiday in the Dominican Republic when Sarah's mother phoned with the news that a large site with planning permission for a detached dwelling was for sale by sealed bids. "We knew the 14th century barn and old farmyard set in seven acres, and decided there and then without hesitation, that we would make a bid whilst we were abroad," Sarah continues.

After successfully purchasing the land, she and Stephen sold their Victorian house and moved into rented accommodation with their two children — later living in a large mobile home on the site for almost four months. "Life in the mobile home started out as an adventure and became a bit of a chore, as we had only packed enough things for a short stay," Stephen explains.

"I don't think that we would have considered building our own home without the help of my brother, Nat, who is an architect. We wanted something modern and innovative, and I took two years off from working as a lecturer in beauty therapy in order to give the project my full attention," says Sarah, who decided to enrol in a design course at Brighton University to gain a greater understanding of the project.

"Nat is thirteen years older than I am, which meant that we were at very different stages in life when we were growing up," Sarah explains. "This project has given us a chance to spend time together, and we would meet two or three times each week and speak on the phone every day. It was fantastic because we had such similar ideas, and I felt extremely privileged to be able to have that time with him."

Self-build is quite obviously in the blood, as both Sarah and Stephen's parents have built their own homes. "We lived abroad, and my parents built a very modern house in Fiji," says Sarah. "Although we had our traumas, Stephen and I found the whole process extremely exciting — being able to design a house exactly to our family's requirements."

Sarah and Stephen had regular design meetings with Nat, who drew up a detailed brief based on their requirements — including a mezzanine overlooking the sitting room, which gives Sarah a private study area with fine views, with a separate TV and hi-fi room helping to define public and more private spaces. "It was extraordinary just how alike our opinions were," says Nat. "I don't think we fell out over anything important."

Sarah and Stephen wanted underfloor heating, a system for collecting rainwater from the roof and storing it for use ▶

"The building [has] a simple form externally.
The notion of surprise was key to the whole concept."

▲ Lighting was an important consideration, and a Lutron computerised lighting system has been preset for a variety of effects and moods, whilst an integrated hi-fi system allows music to be played in every room.

The chapel- ▶ like double height sitting room has a curved ceiling, with panels of glazing giving views of the countryside and lake.

in the bathrooms, and a laundry chute from the bedrooms down to a basement uility room. "I was dubious about constructing a basement at first," says Sarah, "but Stephen felt that it would be perfect for containing all the service areas — and it has proved invaluable for hiding boilers and the laundry room."

The house has been built on the site of an old farmhouse which burned down 20 years before, with the new property positioned adjacent to the existing barn in order to benefit from maximum sunlight, and to take advantage of views towards the lake and fields beyond.

Externally, 'Big Edgerley' itself resembles a timber clad barn with giant entrance doors, and is clearly visible from a well used public footpath. Even though the planning officer and the majority of the planning committee supported this design it still took almost a year to develop the brief and gain full planning permission for the house.

While they waited, Sarah and Stephen spent time dredging the lake and restoring the existing barn as a store and garage. "We then went on to use the same builder who had worked on the barn to build the house," says Stephen.

Archaeologists inspected the site for potential mediaeval remains before the foundations could be dug, with Stephen and Sarah deciding to use some of the spoil to create their own 'mediaeval mound' in the grounds. At this time, bad weather conditions meant that the plot closely resembled a muddy battlefield — with the JCBs struggling to cope. ▶

"We love its spaciousness… and the amount of light which comes in through the large windows."

Built by a ▶ cabinet maker to Sarah and Stephen's linear design, the kitchen features a French limestone floor, teak work surfaces and sliding doors which conceal all the appliances and clutter.

Ease of construction, coupled with the need for large spans, led Nathaniel to specify a prefabricated steel frame – which was erected in just two weeks. Next came the blockwork walling and an external cladding of horizontal iroko weatherboarding, which has been left untreated to weather to a silver grey and blend with the surroundings.

"We asked Nat to design us something which respected its setting and utilised natural materials and local tradesmen wherever possible. Traditional Sussex materials include square knapped flint and stone, with natural slate to the roof," says Sarah. "After much searching for a specialist in knapping – including as far afield as Suffolk – we eventually found a craftsman living locally in West Sussex who knapped all the flints to the front elevation, and laid them between the stone banding."

"To clad the entire building in stone and flint would have been rather extravagant and hugely expensive, and so these materials have been limited to the front facade," Nat explains. "I designed the rectangular building as a simple form externally, giving no clues regarding the circular stairwell and double height spaces inside. The notion of surprise was key to the whole concept."

Windows were also an important factor, with different combinations of square glazing echoed internally with square lights and glass door panels. The master bedroom benefits from a large triangular window above the entrance doors which runs across the full width of the building. ▶

Clad in knapped flint and iroko shiplap, Big Edgerley resembles a simple, rectangular barn.

Fact File costs as of Jan 2003

NAME: Sarah Gee

PROFESSION: Lecturer

AREA: West Sussex

HOUSE TYPE: Five bed detached

HOUSE SIZE: 480m²

BUILD ROUTE: Building contractor

CONSTRUCTION: Steel frame, blockwork, iroko, flint and stone cladding

WARRANTY: Zurich Custom Build

FINANCE: Private

BUILD TIME: 16 months

LAND COST: £250,000

BUILD COST: £470,000

TOTAL COST: £720,000

HOUSE VALUE: £950,000

COST/m²: £979

24% COST SAVING

Cost Breakdown:

Site clearance	£28,300
Foundations and cellar	£75,100
Underground drainage	£17,600
Steel frame	£18,500
Blockwork + brickwork	£23,500
Concrete flooring	£7,200
Iroko cladding	£9,900
Windows, external doors and rooflights	£51,000
Slate roof covering	£23,200
Knapped flintwork and stonework cladding	£16,000
Electrical works	£28,000
Central heating + plumbing	£38,200
Sanitaryware supply	£17,100
Internal doors + joinery	£17,100
Plastering	£14,400
Floor finishes	£22,300
Tiling	£7,600
Lighting + hi-fi system	£29,600
External landscaping	£29,400
TOTAL	**£470,000**

"To me, the view from inside the house is far more important than the appearance of the outside," explains Nathaniel. "Windows have been positioned to maximise the outlook — and the sills on the first floor were set deliberately low to prevent them from dissecting these views, which meant that a metal safety rail was required."

Nathaniel decided that, as a country house, the property should have a grand entrance: oversized 'barn' doors lead into a circular atrium around which the rest of the house is based. A cantilevered limestone staircase is lit from above by a large skylight, whilst the hallway is floored in limestone and provides a perfect space for entertaining.

"I was inspired by a visit to the opera, which featured a dramatic curved staircase on the set," laughs Nat, "and decided that this space should set the tone for the rest of the house. In addition to the aesthetic appeal, the curved stairwell set into a rectangular space left four triangular corners, which were perfect for vertical service runs hiding flues, pipework and the laundry chute."

Sarah sourced many of the materials herself, working closely with Nat on every last detail. "We must have spent five hours just discussing door handles," she laughs. "I searched through adverts in magazines, travelled to London and phoned around to get the best deals. Following the Wembley Stone Show we contacted a French limestone quarry — cutting out the middle man and shipping over our own limestone at a fraction of the retail price. Looking back, the children did grow rather tired of constant discussions about lights and door hinges, although they also got to see a great deal of their uncle.

"Now that we are living in Big Edgerley we love its spaciousness, the underfloor heating and the amount of light which comes in through the large windows — especially in the living room. It is a unique design, tailored specifically to our requirements.." ■

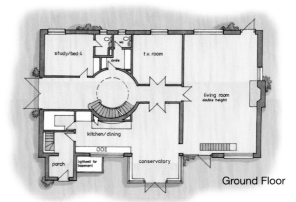

Ground Floor

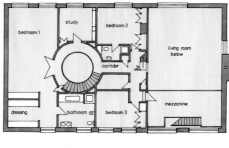

First Floor

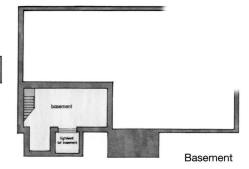

Basement

USEFUL CONTACTS: **Architect** - Nathaniel Gee: 020 7524 7755; **Structural engineer** - Jampel, Davison & Bell: 020 7272 0562; **Main contractor** - Wedgecourt Ltd: 01273 440017; **Structural steelwork** - Prefab Steel Co.: 01273 597733; **Glass & glazing** - The Glass Centre: 01273 776688; **Steel gratings** - Thielco Gratings Ltd: 0208 681 2839; **Sanitaryware** - C P Hart Group: 0207 902 1000; **Knapped flints** - Duncan Berry: 01243 371071; **Joinery & iroko cladding** - Ace Joinery: 01273 439651 **Heating and plumbing engineers** - P J Fraine: 0208 317 9089; **Electricians** - Jarrards Ltd: 01707 262884; **Boilers & central heating pipework** - HCC Systems Ltd: 01400 250572; **Radiators** - Hudevad Britain: 01932 247835; **Electrical faceplates** - Mr Resistor: 020 8874 2234; **Ironmongery** - Laidlaw Ltd: 01223 212567 - Allgood plc: 020 7387 9951; **Hi -fi and Lutron lighting systems** - CCI Ltd: 01903 507077

A BRAND NEW
EXPRESSION

PERGO Expression™ is the latest addition to our collections.
With bevelled edges on all sides, planks in two formats and with an authentic
matching surface structure, you get brand new ways to express yourself.

For a free brochure and nearest stockist,
please call 0800 374771
www.pergo.com

PERGO®
Designed for Generations

GLASS & STEEL

Cutting edge design? In fact this steel and glass edifice is thoroughly 1930s retro — the embodiment of artist Mary Banham's lifelong appreciation of the 'International' style.

Words: **Clive Fewins**   Photography: **Peter Cook**

When artist Mary Banham decided she would like to purchase a house with a studio using the money she gained as a result of selling a house in California she had owned with her late husband, she was keen to achieve a number of things.

At the top of the list were good light and plenty of space. She had been feeling increasingly cramped in the central London flat she shared with her computer consultant son and, since the summer of 1995 when she was given the use of a friend's house in the West Country as a studio for a few weeks, she had yearned for her own studio house in the country.

Although it was not at the top of her mind, as she is now 76 years old, she had considered self-build a distant possibility. She had always wanted to live in a single-storey house and studio in the 'International' style pioneered in the 1930s by her architectural hero, Mies van de Rohe.

As the sun sinks below the ▶ wide horizon of the Fens, the full glory of the simple glass and steel building is revealed. Full height glass walls, strong vertical and horizontal elements and industrial steel structural components are an homage to Mary's architectural hero Ludwig Mies van der Rohe.

◀ The front door is positioned on the east elevation and is accessed by a ramp — a contingency should Mary ever become reliant on a wheelchair.

"I am a great admirer of the Modern Movement so if I was to build, it had to be a single-storey house with a flat roof," Mary said. "Such a house would also need to look right in the landscape. As a painter and writer I feel particularly strongly about this."

Almost to her surprise she has been able to achieve all this in the Fens of Cambridgeshire, thanks to her friendship with architect Jonathan Ellis-Miller and a certain amount of good luck. She had met Cambridge-based Jonathan at an exhibition in London in 1993 and shortly afterwards went to meet him at his house in the Fenland village of Prickwillow, three miles from Ely. As luck would have it, there was a plot of just over a quarter of an acre available next to his house at the very reasonable price of £15,000.

▶

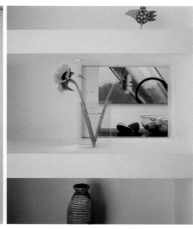

▲ German-made exterior blinds are fixed to a steel overhang. They react according to the wind and the light and can be lowered at night to provide privacy. A photovoltaic cell inside checks the strength of the sun and adjusts the blinds accordingly.

▲ Mary's colourful, non figurative paintings contrast with the simplicity of the plain white walls.

Mary's studio had to ▶ be large enough to accommodate the huge canvasses on which she likes to work. The interior ceiling is of white profiled steel decking apart from one area which is enclosed by a curved clear polycarbonate vaulted roof at the north eastern corner, providing ideal light for an artist.

Jonathan had built his house in 1990. It attracted much attention in the architectural press and won him an RIBA award as well as an award from British Steel for the imaginative use of their materials. His plan was to use his own house as a test bed for other houses in the same Modernist style that he wanted to build.

"The Fenland area suited me because I wanted to be near my daughter who lives in Cambridge," said Mary, who is the widow of Peter Reyner Banham, the distinguished architectural critic and professor of architecture at University College, London. "However, because of my age and my disability — I have only one leg — I did not really consider self-build a serious option."

Another of her requirements was a house that could be built fairly fast. "At the time I was 73 and had lived with a physical disability for more than 40 years," she said. "I felt time was closing in and wanted a house that could double as a studio, that suited my tastes and that was designed to suit my disability. When I sat in Jonathan's house, with its horizontal lines and its slightly industrial look, in the best traditions of the Modern Movement, I fell flat on my face for it, especially in that setting. There is a wonderful feeling of space in the Fens and of course the skies are ideal for painters. It is a landscape with a wonderful spirit of place, in which my spirits go up — a very important factor for someone like me."

She made up her mind in 20 minutes. "It was as if a light went on at the top of my head," she said. "I resolved to go for it, particularly as Jonathan agreed to oversee the project, which we decided to subcontract and run ourselves. I was delighted, as this meant we could get moving fairly fast."

Once the plans had been drawn up and passed, the build took 15 months. Mary moved in last September. The 1,500 sq ft largely open-plan house has one bedroom — though the snug doubles as a guest room and there is an ingenious bathroom arrangement whereby it has two doors and can be approached (and locked) from either side, giving both her and any guests total privacy.

If her children and grandchildren come to stay, they like to occupy the studio space — they love the novelty value of lots of paint around and high ceilings to accommodate the large canvasses she likes to work on.

The house has won a British Steel Award for its design and construction and has a flat steel roof. Its south and west walls are composed almost entirely of large sheets of double glazed, argon filled low-E glass. It is raised up 1.2 metres from the flat ground to give wide views and creates the impression of a building that floats above the Fens.

The front door is positioned by the ramp on the far end of the east elevation. It is deliberately wide to accommodate a wheelchair for Mary, should that ever be necessary in the future. As she is disabled, it is also useful to be able to drive straight up to the door and get out of her car. The other doors are large, single sliding openings in the glazed, south-facing elevation. The most striking views are through the south and east glazed walls across the Fens to Ely Cathedral, rising above the flat landscape on its dry site.

"It is a very site specific house," explained Jonathan. From a distance it looks as if it is floating above the Fens. At night it has the effect of an iridescent glass cube that's just landed from space, particularly as it is lit from below. The views across the Fens are particularly fine when there is a good sunset behind the outline of Ely Cathedral, turning the great gothic building into a rather menacing silhouette."

The German-made exterior blinds drape from the steel overhang, a touch very reminiscent of the architecture of ▶

▲ The core of the house is the bathroom and kitchen in which Mary has used her artistic talent to decorate minimalist wall units. In the background are the vivid blue mdf doors which divide the snug and the bedroom.

Mary was attracted by the quality of the light in the area ▶ which, as an artist, is vital. Clever use of light reflective materials and different textures cause the atmosphere of the house to vary at different times of the day and in different light conditions.

Architect - 01223 359000   **Consulting Engineers** - Hannah Reed: 01223 882000   **Steel frame** - Warboys Services Ltd: 01480 461336   **Underfloor heating** - Thermo floor (GB) Ltd: 01243 822058   **Blinds** - Apex International (UK) Ltd: 0181 838 1113   **Flooring** - Armourex Flowfloor: 01787 248005   **Trombe wall** - Braithwaite Tanks: 01633 262141   **Abbey Glass:** 01284 705500

International Modernist, Mies van de Rohe. They react according to the wind and the light and can be lowered at night and other times to provide privacy. An anemometer mounted high on the south-west corner of the building monitors the wind speed. A photovoltaic cell inside checks the strength of the sun and automatically adjusts the angle of the horizontal blinds accordingly.

The foundations of the house are rafts of concrete on a $4m^2$ grid. From this travel the vertical steel pillars that punctuate the largely open plan interior and support the steelwork of the roof.

> "Residents of a bijou village in the Cotswolds would be up in arms if a house like this was proposed in the village centre and they would have a point."

The core is the bathroom and galley kitchen, created from plasterboard on studwork, with the bedroom located to the south and east of the bathroom and the snug to the south of the kitchen. On the other sides are the open studio area and an airy corridor, surmounted by a curved clear polycarbonate vaulted roof that leads to the enclosed storeroom at the north-east corner of the house.

The glassed wall faces due west over the road to the cathedral across the Fens and a former course of the river Ouse, that can be picked out by a raised row of Poplar trees in the distance. The glass south side, which faces Jonathan's smaller, lower house, is edged with steel decking and steps down. There are large single sliding glass doors at different ends of the south elevation.

The other walls are clad with profiled galvanised sheet steel, known as Colorcoat Pvf2, while the north and east elevations, facing the fringe of the village, are bound by a 2.5m high wall built from reclaimed Cambridge stock bricks. The inner roof is of white profiled steel decking. Above this is 60mm of styrofoam insulation and the outer layer is a single ply waterproof membrane with rainwater collecting channels that drain down towards down pipes at the east end of the building into the storm water drainage system.

"It is one of those quirky oddments in the Fens, of which there are lots – for example, farm and industrial buildings," said Jonathan. "For this reason, the scheme was quite acceptable to local planners. This is a landscape of comparatively new buildings and lightweight, high-tech structures, using modern materials like this house does, fit in well. Four pairs of houses in the council estate up the road, that date from the 1930s, are to be demolished this year. Conventional buildings like this often do not last for ▶

more than a few generations unless they have very carefully engineered foundations, on account of the drying and contracting of the peat in the ground."

Jonathan's own house had proved acceptable to planners 10 years ago, so he could see why there was no objection to Mary's house. "Apart from the fact that it complements the landscape, it is in an ideal site on the edge of the village envelope," he said. "Residents of a bijou village in the Cotswolds would be up in arms if a house like this was proposed in the village centre and they would have a point. But demand nowadays is suggesting that you can get planning permission for this style of house if you are imaginative in your approach and select your location with care."

Inside, a heat-collecting trombe wall behind the glass on the south elevation, is built from concrete cast on site between moulded steel sections. Thermal mass is also provided by the 100mm floor screed. The full-height blue painted doors, which contrast vividly with the all-white walls and ceiling, can be pulled from their normal station covering the trombe wall, to divide the snug and bedroom. Made from mdf with 75mm of insulation inside they create a cosy little room for Mary to relax in beside the open fire, should she want one. The result of all this, plus the passive solar gain and very high levels of insulation, are an SAP rating of 168 and a prediction that heating bills will not exceed £50 per annum.

Overheating in summer can be avoided simply by opening the doors – all three if necessary – to create a through draught. Large cantilevers built from vertical flat plates of steel overhang the house on the south and east sides adding to the effect of the house as a series of planes jutting out and exploring the landscape. On a more practical note they also help counteract overheating in summer. In addition, they provide a diffused effect for the light striking these elevations of the house. The result, together with the effect of the exterior blinds is what Jonathan calls "a play of dappled light on the floors of grey industrial grade epoxy material."

After only a few months of occupancy Mary Banham has no idea yet of how the building and its setting will affect her paintings, which are large, varied in style, not generally naturalistic and favour bright colours. "All I can really say is that I shall do my utmost to produce works worthy of my beautiful house," she said. ■

Fact File costs as of May 1999

NAMES: Mary Banham

PROFESSIONS: Artist and writer

AREA: Cambridgeshire

HOUSE TYPE: Steel frame bungalow

HOUSE SIZE: 139m^2

BUILD ROUTE: Sub contractors

CONSTRUCTION: Steel frame and glass

WARRANTY: Architect's Certificate

BUILD TIME: 15 months (completed September 1998)

LAND COST: £15,000

BUILD COST: £120,000

HOUSE VALUE: £150,000

COST/m^2: £80

11% COST SAVING

Cost Breakdown:

Land	£15,000
Groundworks	£12,000
Steel frame	£22,000
Glass	£20,000
Roof	£12,000
Underfloor heating, plumbing, installation of services	£7,000
Direct labour	£20,000
Brickwork	£10,000
Kitchen	£3,000
Slate hearth and granite worktops	£2,000
Steel flue and chimney	£1,500
Floor and finishing	£1,500
Doors and joinery	£2,500
Bathroom fittings and shower	£2,000
External works	£3,000
Sundries	£1,500
TOTAL	**£120,000**

Mary's floor plan is simple and flowing, making the optimum use of the 1,500 sq ft of space. Recessed sliding doors, made from sheets of mdf sandwiching 75mm of insulation, can be drawn to screen off a cosy seating area within the main gallery, thus allowing flexible use of the space.

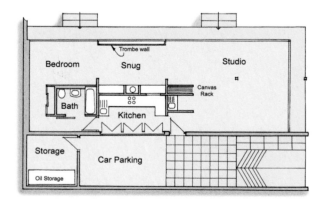

◀ Tucked away at the edge of the village, Mary's house echoes the form of industrial buildings in the area. Jonathan Ellis-Miller set the pattern for buildings of this sort in the area with his own award winning home.

Second Nature
Kitchen Collection

Made to Measure

A contemporary home for a narrow urban site

Terry and Gilly Pawson have built a spectacular contemporary style four storey home on a narrow urban site.

Words:
Debbie Jeffery
Photography:
Richard Bryant

Predominantly ▶
timber and brick,
the house
deliberately
reflects the
traditional
materials of the
area — but they
have been
applied in a
contemporary
way.

If the Pawson house needed to be summed up in just three words, they would be: tall, light and handsome. Due to the restricted nature of its site, this innovative building is only one room wide and very tall — which is something of an oddity for a property newly constructed within a conservation area in Wimbledon. With the current trend for present-day housing to appear subservient to its period predecessors, planners are usually adamant that newly-built homes keep a low profile.

The site may have dictated the design parameters, but it also brought with it a whole series of construction dilemmas. "When we purchased our house we were aware that the property had been underpinned by a previous owner under an insurance cover," Terry Pawson explains. Despite this problem, he and his wife Gilly were attracted by the mature gardens, pleasant location and small price tag, and lived in the converted coach house with their two sons before realising that the cause of the subsidence had not been rectified.

"No-one knew that an extensive land drain ran below the property, which was broken and had continued to leak. Deepening the foundations in the clay soil had done nothing to alleviate this problem."

Ultimately, the family decided that the small brick cottage would have to be demolished and a replacement house constructed. With no insurance pay-out, they had a relatively tight budget and an extremely tight site. "It wasn't an ideal scenario," Terry continues, "but we had to make the best of the situation and start again."

The two storey cottage occupied a long thin strip of land on the east facing slope of the ridge that runs right across Wimbledon. At five metres wide, the site is actually narrower than an average three bedroom terraced house, but extends to some 80m in length. A mature oak tree, the unusual proportions of the plot and its prominent position among imposing 1900s villas have all influenced the final design.

"We approached the planners very early on to discuss the various issues," says Terry. "There were a lot of consultations but, from day one, they were very positive and supportive. We never asked for anything unreasonable which could not be justified, and the response from the officers was encouraging."

▶

The exposed concrete staircase with its slim handrail provides a dramatic feature in the toplit hallway, which is filled with natural light.

With the building only one room wide, a feeling of complexity has been created within the section of the house. The interior deliberately plays with the perception of space: compressing and then opening out in an unexpected direction to create a series of changing volumes, with sunlight penetrating into every corner.

An oak clad tower sits on a reinforced concrete base, and has a bedroom and bathroom on each of its four floors, whilst a brick cube holds the stairs. Living spaces have been positioned beneath a planted, vaulted roof, and are able to open out fully onto the garden – blurring the division between inside and out. Each space has a different aspect: from the skylit hall to the rooftop terrace, set amongst the upper branches of the oak tree.

Terry – principal of Terry Pawson Architects – decided that this project would provide the opportunity to act as architect, client and main contractor – allowing him the freedom to explore new ideas and construction techniques.

"I was responsible for all aspects of the building design, procurement and funding," he says. "The building was constructed over an extended period of time, using a combination of direct labour and specialist contractors. This provided the opportunity to develop details on site from a practical, rather than a theoretical viewpoint, and to be actively involved and personally fabricate some elements of the house. Although I had never really tackled anything like this before, I helped to put up the timber structure and partitioning, decorated and generally laboured on site where I could."

This approach meant that the project management was carried out on a part-time basis at weekends and early mornings – a necessary consequence of the constraints on both time and finance. Terry admits that more time spent on the issue of purchasing materials would have improved the overall efficiency of the process, but feels that the experience allowed him to develop a better understanding of a self-build project.

"We put our furniture into storage and moved in with my mother during the build," says Gilly, a curate. "The whole process has taken four years, and was prolonged ▶

Set more than 3 metres below the level of the road and entrance hall, the kitchen is contained within a concrete 'box'.

The steep ▶ concrete staircase has an almost sculptural form, with Gilly's own sculptures featuring in the hallway.

"The very constraints have ultimately led to a much more interesting building"

because Terry was also setting up a new practice during this time. For almost a year we did nothing about the house. I think the neighbours were extremely glad when we finally finished!"

Structurally, the building comprises three distinct components: a concrete podium ground floor and basement; a timber framed superstructure to the front three storeys and a steel framed external envelope enclosing the main double height spaces to the rear.

"Terry wanted a simple form to unify the lower ground floor spaces and link with the upper storeys using a central staircase," says structural engineer, Bob Barton. "Concrete seemed the obvious choice and, given the concern about the site's settlement problems, we decided to use a reinforced concrete structure throughout — including the ground floor. This was designed to be a watertight box, which also acts as a damp proofing system. All the concrete elements were constructed in one phase, creating the locally renowned sight: 'the staircase sculpture'!"

A simple platform frame system was used for the three storey bedroom tower, with timber stud walls and a timber joisted floor. This has been clad externally in oak boarding, whilst the central circulation space was to be clad in brick. Here, an intricate steel frame was devised which was carefully integrated into the fabric of the external walls, and accommodates the glass slots and recesses in the ground floor storey. The steel solution was also used for the low-level rear extension, which steps down the slope of the garden. ▶

The wall between the dining room and garden can be folded back, so that this double height room opens directly onto the terrace, with a full height void between the hall and kitchen bringing light into this section of the interior. The glazing has a slight green tint.

Internally, the finish materials are restricted to white painted walls, with floors of either oak or black slate. Elements of the structural in-situ concrete are also left exposed, principally in the main staircase and the concrete platform set above the kitchen — on which the upper ground floor sitting room is positioned. This has a barrel vaulted roof, glass balustrade and overlooks the mature gardens to the rear.

"Nobody would choose to build on such a difficult site," says Terry. "But the very constraints have ultimately led to a much more interesting building which responds directly to its location and yet feels spacious and generous inside.

"I'm extremely pleased with the quality of natural light within the house and the way the building connects to the garden. It has taken time, but we have learnt a great deal from building our own home and are now simply enjoying living here." ∎

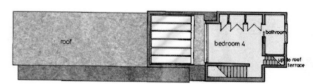

Third Floor

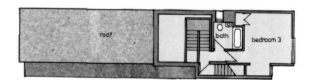

Second Floor

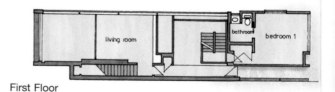

First Floor

Fact File costs as of Feb 2003

NAMES: Terry and Gilly Pawson

PROFESSIONS: Architect & Curate

AREA: South West London

HOUSE TYPE: 4 bedroom detached

HOUSE SIZE: 186m²

BUILD ROUTE: Subcontractors + self

CONSTRUCTION: Concrete, timber, steel + brick

FINANCE: NatWest loan

BUILD TIME: Three years

LAND COST: £200,000

BUILD COST: £320,000

TOTAL COST: £520,000

65% COST SAVING

HOUSE VALUE: £1.5m+

COST/m²: £1,720

Cost Breakdown:

Concrete, groundworks + drainage £55,000

Steel frame £10,000

Timber frame/cladding £21,000

Roof coverings/flashings £8,000

Windows and glazing £26,000

Heating and plumbing £13,000

Electrical and lighting £4,000

Sanitaryware £6,000

Building work £143,000

Landscaping £3,000

Kitchen £7,000

Doors and ironmongery £7,000

Timber + slate floor finishes . .£17,000

TOTAL £320,000

USEFUL CONTACTS: **Architect** – Terry Pawson Architects: 020 8543 2577 www.terrypawson. com; **Structural Engineer** – Barton Engineers: 020 7928 9099; **Timber supply** – Chelsea Timber Merchants Ltd: 0208 7700448; **Bricks** – Baggeridge Brick PLC: 01902 880666; **Oak cladding** – Layton Timber: 01491 613222; **Stainless steel cladding fixings** – Stainless Threaded Fasteners Ltd: 01902 490490; **Glass and glazing** – Compass Glass & Glazing Ltd: 020 8946 8080; **Sliding windows, rooflight** – Sunfold Systems: 01362 699744; **Louvre windows** – Ruskin Air Management Ltd: 0151 527 2525; **Underfloor heating** – Eurogauge Co Ltd: 01342 323641; **Planted vaulted roof** – Index Building Products Ltd: 020 7409 7151; **External paints** – Keim Mineral Paints Ltd: 01746 714543; **Ironmongery** – Hafele UK Ltd: 01788 542020; **Slate flooring** – Kirkstone Quarries Ltd: 01539 433296; **Glass mosaic tiles** – Edgar Udny and Co: 020 8767 8181; **Lighting** – Concord Lighting Ltd: 01273 515811; **Insurance** - DMS Services: 01909 591652

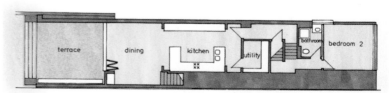

Ground Floor

FLOORPLAN: To take advantage of the narrow sloping site the ground floor spaces have been lowered using a reinforced concrete box structure. The four bedrooms and bathrooms are contained within the four storey oak clad tower at the front, topped off with a roof terrace. The living rooms and kitchen have been positioned in the two storey steel framed section to the rear.

for those in the home improvement market, here is a new opportunity for you

in-doors

t: +44 (0)1362 699744
f: +44 (0) 1362 698787
e: indoors@sunfold.com
w: www.sunfold.com

Sunfold Systems Ltd

t: +44 (0)1362 699744
f: +44 (0)1362 698787
e: info@sunfoldsystems.co.
w: www.sunfold.com

Contemporary Country

Building an innovative modern house on a budget

An award-winning new home in Perthshire shows how high architecture
doesn't necessarily have to mean high build costs.

As if winning the RIBA award for best First Building by
a New Practice at the 2001 Stirling Prize wasn't
enough, Mark Walker's self-designed home, Cedar
House, also features as an exemplar of rural housing in the
new Scottish Executive's Policy on Architecture. All of
which isn't bad at all considering the total build cost of
this landscape hugging, contemporary style family home
was little over £127,000, or just over £500/m².

Mark and Chloe Walker and family moved up to rural
Perthshire from London ten years ago. Architect Mark,
who currently teaches architecture at the Edinburgh
College of Art, had been keen to build in Scotland as well
as teach but the opportunity hadn't quite presented itself.
That is, until Chloe was left a legacy of £150,000 which
the couple promptly set aside to buy a plot of land and
design and build a new family home.

Words:
Caroline Ednie

Photography:
Andrew Lee

►

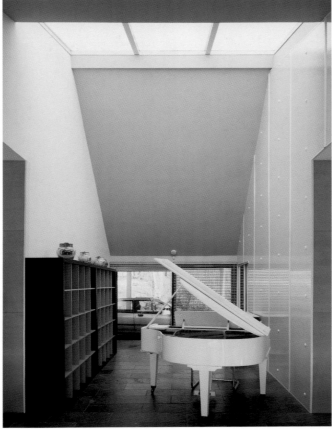

Finding a suitable plot proved difficult. The Walkers had a bit of a break however, as Mark explains. "Planning permission generally doesn't encourage individual houses in Scotland. We were lucky, however, as we managed to hear from a friend of ours that a prime site from the Scone Estate was being put on the market."

So, snapping up this half acre chunk of rolling Glenalmond, it only remained for the planning process to kick in, which according to Mark "has a tendency in Scotland to favour copies of older traditional forms than more contemporary buildings." However the rigorous environmental and ecological design presented by Walker Architecture won a great deal of support from the planning officer who was dealing with the site, and to Mark's relief the challenging stylistic proposals were also embraced. In fact, the precedent set by this particularly enlightened planner has, says Mark, precipitated a response from the Scottish Executive to encourage local authorities in rural areas to be less conservative in their approach to planning.

Now that the obstacles were cleared Walker Architecture could then get on with the "challenge of building something that is not pastiche traditional architecture or a nostalgia for country living," but an elegant contemporary response to the glorious Perthshire setting.

In terms of design this single storey, four bedroom family home is simplicity itself. Planned on a grid and on top ▶

The internal ▶ layout is based around one open plan living space which has loosely defined functions.

The bedrooms and bathrooms are connected by an enclosed corridor which is lit from above via the glazed roof. ▶

of a foundation of concrete poured in trenches, a timber box was constructed using double sections of 6 inch by 2 inch timber. On to this the roof trusses were positioned. Walls were filled with insulation and then clad externally. The overall effect is like a "packing crate" as Mark calls it.

With the exception of the north facing bedrooms and internal double garage, the exterior walls are timber framed sliding doors, glazed with low-emissivity glass. The crisp transparency of these glass walls is balanced by the warm cedar cladding of the gables and boards above the patio doors as well as the western red cedar shingles of the low pitch asymmetrical roof. This affords the home its unmistakably rural feel, which appears almost like a Modernist barn.

Mark's decision to create a simple monolithic shell by "cutting away frilly details and embellishments such as projecting roofs and porches," also meant that there would be more money to spend on high quality materials. So, in addition to the red cedar cladding and roof shingles, which Mark claims will only improve with age and weathering, interior walls are lined with birch faced plywood, and floors are finished in reclaimed oak and Brazilian Rio Ferrada slate. To complete the picture of opulence, custom made Woodslat blinds line the glazed walls, and when

"The important thing is the fact that good architecture needn't necessarily be really expensive and the Cedar House prototype does give people some confidence that it can be done…"

closed at night "simulate the effect of a very warm and glowing box," according to Mark.

The quality of interior space is as top notch as the materials. Mark defines these spaces in terms of 'day' and 'night' areas. The 'day' areas, which are arranged along a cruciform layout, begin via a roomy entrance hall on the short axis, which opens up into a light and airy open plan living and dining area occupying the central axis. Following the line of the main south facing glazed wall leads to a long and luxuriously fitted kitchen complete with combination oven and halogen hobs. All services are contained within a semi-transparent polycarbonate 'wall,' which backs on to the double bathroom. The 'day' area culminates in a compact office annex, which Mark claims he would have extended if the site had allowed.

A series of internal 'night' spaces are enclosed within the north face of the house. Four bedrooms facing two identical bathrooms are connected by a top lit corridor and, being contained underneath the lowest trajectory of

The corridor kitchen has cupboard doors supplied by Swan Robes (01259 762669) and worktops by flooring specialists Junckers. ◀

the sloping roof, the bedrooms especially have a cosiness and intimacy which contrasts effectively with the open plan 'day' areas.

According to Mark, "economical planning and not having any redundant spaces" was pivotal in keeping the budget costs in check. "The actual economy of the building is that I absolutely reduced the circulation space. For example, although there is a corridor linking the bedrooms and bathrooms, it's as straight and small as it could be. It's also 1500mm wide so it feels like a room, and could potentially be a library.

"There is also a virtual economy in the house, in that it feels a lot bigger than it is. For example, the device of the big mirror on the living area wall doubles the space, and the south east wall of the entrance hall is clad in 16mm triple walled polycarbonate, which creates a translucent internal screen rather than a solid wall."

Cedar House's energy efficient approach also makes economic sense. A steady temperature is achieved by an ▶

USEFUL CONTACTS: **Architect** – Walker Architecture: 01738 880419 **UFH** – Invisible Heating Systems: 01854 613161 **Contractor** – B & B Tealing **Woodslat Blinds** – Chris Craft: 01356 625111 **Western red cedar shingles** – Loft Shop: 0870 6040404 **Rio Ferrada slate floor** – Kirkstone Quarries: 01539 433296 **Wood burning stove** – LHA: 0151 625 0504 **Patio doors and windows** – Allan Brothers: 01289 334600 **Sanitaryware** – Ideal Standard:01482 346461**Garage doors** – Hormann garage door company: 01467 632178 **Boiler** – Delta F45 HR by ACV: 01383 820100 **Kitchen worktop** – Junkers: 01376 534700 **Cupboard doors** – Swan Robes 01259 762669 **Coir mat** – Mat Services: 01568 616642 **Worktops** – Junkers: 01376 534700

underfloor heating system in the form of water pipes embedded into the concrete floor. This is fired by an oil fueled boiler which sits in a cupboard next to the master bedroom. Mark admits this would have been better located in the garage as it makes a noise "a bit like a jet engine." Then there is the solar gain, which in this case is considerable, due to the predominance of glazed facades. As if all this weren't enough a Scan wood burning stove is also on hand if an extra boost is needed.

It's hardly surprising then that the house has now become something of a prototype for rural housing. And although Mark clearly "didn't have this intention when I built it originally," the simple modular and economical model made so much sense that a number of prospective clients throughout the UK and Ireland began to beat a path to Cedar House, to see what they could get for themselves in terms of affordable cutting edge design.

So, with the benefit of hindsight, will Mark be approaching the Cedar House progeny any differently? Well, for one thing he is determined that the construction process won't be the same next time round. "With Cedar House," he explains, "I did a set of drawings, and sourced and priced much of the materials (patio doors, slate floor, stove, kitchen, blinds), but didn't want to manage the project myself. I was trying to find a contractor who would do everything and I did eventually find someone but they had only been used to producing the same house over and over again and were not really geared up for this new challenge. I think perhaps I got into bed with the wrong people.

"I would now tackle the project acting as an architect, and would stipulate a more closely written contract. In Cedar House it was just an exchange of letters."

Consequently, the Cedar House project took around a year, when it should have taken around 12 to 16 weeks, which is what Mark is aiming for with the Cedar House prototype he is building for clients in Peebles in the Scottish Borders. "They're taking the same external envelope and wall of glass whilst making a few modifications outside. Internally, however, they've requested a separate garage and a big utility room and three instead of four bedrooms. There are many options in the modular system. The scale, structure and the idea however, are all the same.

"The important thing," Mark says, "is the fact that good architecture needn't necessarily be really expensive and the Cedar House prototype does give people some confidence that it can be done." ■

FLOORPLAN: For economy circulation space is kept to an absolute minimum. The only corridor, linking the bedrooms and bathrooms, is 1500mm wide and could be used as a library.

Fact File costs as of Sept 2002

NAMES: Mark & Chloe Walker

PROFESSIONS: Architects

AREA: Perthshire

HOUSE TYPE: Four bed detached

HOUSE SIZE: 228m²

BUILD ROUTE: Main Contractor

CONSTRUCTION: Timber frame

WARRANTY: NHBC

SAP RATING: 83

FINANCE: Private

BUILD TIME: Jan '99 – Jan '00

LAND COST: £43,000	47%
BUILD COST: £127,000	COST SAVING
TOTAL COST: £170,000	

HOUSE VALUE: £315,000

COST/m²: £558

Cost Breakdown:

Main contract	.£110,855
UFH	.£5,060
Blinds	.£5,553
TV Aerial	.£189
Fencing and gates	.£555
Floor mats	.£179
Tarmac Drive	.£1,996
Floor seal	.£244
TOTAL	**£127,300**

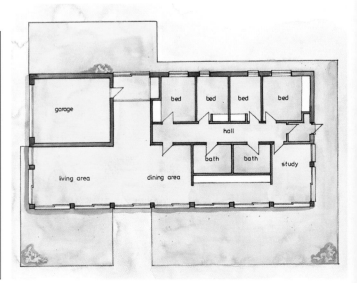

Ray of Light

Peter Cookson Smith and Alison Thompson have created an exciting new home in steel and glass on the banks of the River Thames near Richmond.

Words:
Jude Webley

Photography:
Dennis Gilbert/VIEW

Compared to the typical self-build project, building a radical contemporary style home in steel and glass on the bank of the River Thames is a whole new ball game. Put away your average build cost tables and any talk of using directly employed subcontractors — this project is about top quality design from one of the UK's leading architectural practices, Edward Cullinan Architects, and the complex process of turning design concepts into beautifully crafted and detailed reality.

Peter Cookson Smith is an architect himself, working on large scale infrastructure projects. He and partner Alison Thompson had been living and working overseas in Hong Kong but planned to return to the UK. Peter had snapped up the fantastic plot overlooking the Thames some years before. Following the erection of a new flood wall, some plots of land adjacent to the riverbank that previously flooded became suitable for development. Peter and Alison wanted to build something special and contemporary that would require the inspiration of not just an architect, but an artist. ▶

Building a

radical contemporary home

The couple commissioned the Cullinan practice to come up with a design study. The brief called for a house containing a variety of spaces for quiet study, relaxation, entertainment and all of the other normal domestic requirements. They wanted a design that would make best use of the fantastic river views and allow in as much light as possible but without sacrificing privacy.

The initial design study met with client approval but, predictably, failed to win planning consent. It subsequently took a great deal of determination and a refusal to admit defeat to get this proposal accepted.

"The original consent on the plot was for a small cottage," recalls project architect Peter Inglis. "This consent had lapsed but the planners did not seem that keen to discuss new proposals for the site. Our application was refused, principally on the grounds that it was detrimental to a line of sycamore trees.

"You have to be prepared, as in this case, to appeal… Otherwise you'll end up listening to what they say they want and end up with a house like everyone else's."

"Fortunately the client, who had previously worked in planning himself, decided to appeal. He hired a firm of planning consultants who produced a lengthy document showing, amongst other things, that the trees would be able to survive and prosper alongside the proposed house." In March 1998, two years after work started on the design, the planning inspector accepted the appeal and work could start in earnest.

"A lot of people lie down and wiggle their legs in the air when the planners turn down their proposal," comments the contractor, Paul Gilby of Gilby Construction. "If you want to build something unusual and challenging in this country my advice is to put a great deal of effort into choosing the right architect and then keep faith with him. You have to be prepared, as in this case, to appeal against planning decisions and let the planners know you will go all the way. Otherwise you'll end up listening to what they say they want and end up with a house like everyone else's."

The design of both house and garden, starting at the roadside and going right through to the riverside, was based on a grid of multiples of 1200mm. A great deal of care was taken with the setting out of the project on site to ensure that each element of the design related correctly to the rest. The buildings, composed of London stock brick, western red cedar, and zinc cladding, are set back from the road to provide an open area for two car parking spaces together with an entrance drive. An elevated entrance extends through the internal entrance hall and beyond as an external timber deck. This is set back from

the edge of the site in order to retain the existing trees along the boundary (in tune with the planners' wishes) but gives a clear and uninterrupted view of the river from the entrance itself. On the river side of the house is a private garden. This includes the raised timber deck which steps up to "oversail" the existing floodwall leading to a (yet to be constructed) river mooring.

The internal planning of the main house is ordered around a curving wall, which incorporates stairs, storage and display cases and provides vantage points throughout the house from which to enjoy framed views across the river. The large expanse of glazing can be shaded when required by external timber blinds which are operated by an electric motor. This system of environmental control was partially developed for the project.

Heating is provided by warm water underfloor heating from Thermoboard and cooling can be assisted by natural ventilation provided by high and low level opening windows which are again motorised. The building services ▶

Because of the ▷ large expanse of glazing the solid structural walls were super-insulated to 0.18W/m²K.

engineer who designed the heating system ran a computer modelling programme to predict the effect of solar gain (natural warming from the sun) on the house. Because of the large expanse of glazing the solid structural walls were super-insulated to a far better than building regs U–value of $0.18W/m^2K$ as a trade off so that the structure as a whole attained an acceptable SAP rating.

"Instead of operating in what often turns out to be an adversarial way with the contractor, we wanted to partner with him and use his expertise."

Gilby Construction had been brought in at an early stage at the suggestion of the quantity surveyor. "In the practice generally we've not been happy with the standard ways of procuring buildings," comments Peter Inglis. "Instead of operating in what often turns out to be an adversarial way with the contractor we wanted to partner with him and use his expertise.   ▷

Useful Contacts

Architect — Edward Cullinan Architects (Peter Inglis): 0207 704 1975

Structural Engineer — John Romer of Edward Cullinan Architects: 0207 704 1975

Quantity Surveyor — Peter Gittins & Associates: 020 8948 4544

Contractor — Gilby Construction: 0207 394 9444

Landscape — Derek Lovejoy Partnership: 020 7828 6392

Steel Frame/Metalwork/Staircases — John Rich Fabrications: 01795 591178

Infill Framing — Metsec: 0121 552 1541

Windows — Timber/Aluminium Composite Windows — Velfac Ltd: 01223 426606

Steel Sliding and Curved Entrance Doors — Vista Brunswick: 0117 955 1491

Breathing Membrane — Tyvek www.tyvek.com

Insulation — Rockwool:01656 862621

Roofing — Rheinzink: 01276 686725

Timber External Blinds — Taurus Littrow: 01949 836600

Patterned Glass — Saint Gobain: 024 7654 7400

Kitchen Manufacturer — Euromobil; Supplier/Fitter: BK Barget: 020 7376 1444

Built-in furniture, doors etc. — Lignum Vitae Cabinetmakers: 020 8965 8839

Wooden Flooring — Junckers: 01376 517512

Ironmongery — Allgood: 020 7387 9951

Sliding doorgear/patch fittings — Dorma: 01462 472502

WCs and Sinks — Villeroy & Boch: 020 8871 0011

Glass Sink — CP Hart: 020 7902 1000

Taps — Vola: 01525 841155

Bath and Shower — Ucosan: 01625 52 52 02

Tiles — Shackerley Ltd: 01257 273114

Uplights and Downlights — Concord: 01273 515811

Floor lights in Entrance — Lois Poulsen: 01372 848800

Underfloor Heating — Thermoboard: 01392 444122

Trench Heaters — Kampmann: 020 8783 0033

Fireplaces — Croydon Fireplaces: 020 8684 1495

▲ The steel staircases were fabricated to working drawings by John Rich Fabrications (01795 591178). The timber flooring is from Junckers.

Fact File costs as of Dec 2001

NAME: Peter Cookson Smith and Alison Thompson

PROFESSIONS: Architect and Coroner

AREA: West London

HOUSE TYPE: Contemporary

HOUSE SIZE: 377m²

BUILD ROUTE: Architect/Quantity Surveyor/Main Contractor

CONSTRUCTION: Steel frame + in-situ cast waterproof concrete basement

WARRANTY: Architect's Certificates

SAP RATING: Not known

FINANCE: Private

BUILD TIME: Two years

LAND COST: Undisclosed

BUILD COST: £900,000

CURRENT VALUE: £3-4m

COST/m²: £2,387

Cost Breakdown:

Enabling work:	£25,000
Substructure/Basement:	£155,333
Steel Frame:	£34,998
External Walls and Joinery	£29,646
Windows/Blinds/ External Doors	£63,602
Upper floors:	£20,022
Roofs:	£47,882
Internal Walls:	£49,093
Staircases:	£53,900
Internal Doors:	£4,675
Wall, Ceiling, Floor Finishes:	£26,814
Sanitary/Kitchen/ Built-in Fittings:	£110,482
M&E, Plumbing, Electrics:	£72,984
Landscape/External Works:	£43,300
TOTAL	**£900,000**

"Paul Gilby's firm had special expertise in piling, steelwork and waterproof concrete techniques to bring to the project. We wanted to get him involved in the detailed design stage and with implementing our rolling cost plan along with the QS."

Paul Gilby takes up the story. "We're very rarely on tender lists since we normally refuse to tender. On this job we were presented with 1:100 planning drawings and a cost plan from the QS with a series of budgets to work to. It's important that there are realistic expectations. We also have to check that the skill base required for a particular job is available at the right time as we will only work with subcontractors whose work we know and trust.

> "We can advise people how to achieve the shape of the building they want for the money they have..."

"Cost planning is everything. If we're involved early we can advise against overspecification in some areas if it's going to mean the budget won't work. We can advise people how to achieve the shape of the building they want for the money they have. We came up with a method statement of how the house was going to be built, in a lot of detail, and then provided fixed prices for every element and a fixed contract period. On this job we were able to advise on how best to achieve the brief for the available budget. Really this was a pretty straightforward project making sensible use of available technologies."

The structural frame of the house is formed in cold rolled steel, infilled with Metsec stud partitioning with 9mm OSB board, Rockwool roll insulation, Tyvec membrane and vapour check, plywood clad on the exterior with western red cedar and London stock brick. Once the steel frame had gone up the project was weathertight in a week. The only slow part was the brick wall (the planners insisted on some "wattle and daub," says Gilby sarcastically).

On the roof rolled steel T-sections followed the roll of the roof and were fixed to the primary cross steels. Timber joists were then fitted from left to right, again following the curve of the roof, overlaid with planks of pine, two layers of Rockwool Rainscreen Duo (as well as thermal insulation this product provided acoustic shielding from the sound of rain drumming on the roof), a Tyvek membrane and a RheinZink roof.

According to the contractor, the most challenging part of the job was in the ground. Due to the ground conditions, piled foundations were necessary, plus Peter and Alison wanted a full basement for storage and to house the boiler and so on. There was only 30mm of clearance on one pile from a neighbour's fence.

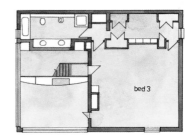

Second Floor

Since the plot is so close to the Thames the water table rises and falls by 2ft according to the tide. Being experienced in waterproof concrete technology Gilby took responsibility for the waterproofing of the basement. No tanking was used. The walls were formed from in situ poured concrete using a special formula concrete vibrated in a particular way with chemical water bars. "Because of the tide we had to be really careful with the timing of concrete deliveries," explains Paul.

How did this all work with the client thousands of miles away in Hong Kong? "The detail design stage was all done by fax," says Peter Inglis. "The client responded very quickly and it all went very smoothly, in spite of the distance. When it came to selecting the materials we used to get samples of everything in the office and the client would come and inspect a batch on one of his trips to London. On site, as always, there were plenty of decisions that needed taking and the client was always fully involved."

The project was run on a standard JCT IFC98 contract for intermediate value projects administered by the architect. ■

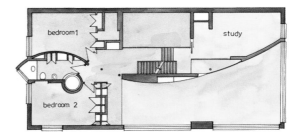

First Floor

The buildings, composed of London stock brick, western red cedar, and zinc cladding, are set back from the road to provide an open area for two car parking spaces together with an entrance drive.

Ground Floor

Urban Vision

Jeremy Till and Sarah Wigglesworth have created a landmark postmodern home in a prominent position.

Words:
Clive Fewins

Photography:
Philip Bier/ViEW

With its timber-clad tower and gaunt-looking exterior wall of sandbags, the window openings formed from railway sleepers found on site, the new north London home of home of Jeremy Till and Sarah Wigglesworth could almost be mistaken for some kind of penal institution. At least this is how it might appear to rail travellers just gathering speed as they pass by on one of the main lines out of the capital.

However, this is just one elevation. The others contain all manner of materials, from plywood to corrugated steel, polycarbonate, lime render, yew, cedar boarding, wire mesh, zinc, and a silvery cladding that looks like a duvet that has been squashed, puckered and buttoned.

With such a wacky list of materials it is small wonder that the house, for which they gained their planning permission at the first attempt within seven weeks, is rapidly becoming a landmark for rail travellers leaving Kings Cross station, a mile down the line.

"The outer covering of the sand bags will eventually decay and the contents – sand, cement and lime – will ▶

**The cladding ▶
on the elevations
captures a range
of different
building
materials, from
straw to glass, all
based around a
steel frame.**

90

some trainspotting — or even fall asleep. "The staircase has treads of various depths to make it easy to sit on and is provided with cushions for when a spontaneous dip into a book turns into something more compelling," Sarah explains.

Although they plan to finish the tower, Sarah and Jeremy see other areas of the house as remaining "permanently incomplete" as they put it. "Being designers we continually like to tweak things," Sarah adds.

One of the most dazzling complete sections is the kitchen. The huge central larder – they call it the "beehive" – goes up to ceiling height and is the undoubted focal point of this area of the house as well as the means of separating the kitchen area from the living room. Another memorable feature is the dining corner with its built-in seats, reflected on the outside by layers of more horizontal cedar cladding that splays out in a series of overhangs. The table is made of a vast number of pieces of coloured broken glass cast using a resin process developed by colleagues at Sheffield Hallam University. It projects through the wall to the deck, which is above the entrance vestibule and faces south-west for outdoor eating.

The "beehive" is modelled on mud structures found in many eastern countries. It is wrapped in mineral fibre insulation, covered in a galvanised mesh and coated with a coarse lime plaster. The effect is to make it wonderfully sculptural and tactile. It projects through the roof and is vented from the outside.

At the other side of the double height living room with its 'floating' mezzanine floor you reach a blank timber wall faced with douglas fir plywood. This can be slid back to reveal a six metre high banqueting area that joins the domestic with the working area of the building. This dual function room doubles as dining room and a conference room both for Sarah's architectural practice and also for the other architectural practice that shares the work area.

You pass through this to the office space proper. This comprises 150 of the 425m^2 total build area. It begins at first floor level, and is supported by concrete pillars surrounded by large gabion baskets. Made of heavy-duty galvanised steel wire they are commonly used to prevent erosion in river banks and supporting areas of motorway embankment. They contain lumps of recycled concrete.

"Before the introduction of Landfill Tax, construction waste accounted for 30 per cent of all waste in the UK. We wanted to make the point that a lot of these materials can be reused and also make a few suggestions as to how city dwellers can reduce the environmental impact of the buildings they live in," Jeremy says.

When trains pass by you often feel a slight 'wobble.' This is because the work and main living areas are perched on springs, based on columns. This is the reason for the two other most unusual features – the staircase on wheels and the bridge between the upstairs of the bedroom wing, ▶

"When trains pass by you often feel a slight wobble. This is because the work and main living areas are perched on springs, based on columns…"

The huge ▲ larder, which Sarah and Jeremy call the "beehive", separates the kitchen from the living room.

One of the ▶ most dramatic rooms in the house is the six metre high dining hall, which is also used as a conference room.

form a wall of rippling, uneven concrete with a rough imprint of the cloth covering on the exterior," says Jeremy, who is head of the School of Architecture at the University of Sheffield. "The railway elevation is deliberately designed to be seen from a passing train with the random scattering of openings intended to confuse the sense of scale and place as train passengers look up from their papers and see this strange sight."

It is not the only 'fun' element – designed to amuse as well as confuse – which the two have built into the house, which is in part an experiment to test the ideas of Jeremy and Sarah, also an architect and academic. From the top of the tower, clad in horizontal cedar boarding, you get not only a good view of surrounding Holloway but also the rest of the house, complete with sloping turf roof, and also of how the astonishing array of materials interact with one another.

The tower is not yet finished. Eventually it will house Sarah and Jeremy's library. The plan is to have books lining the walls all the way up. The rooftop retreat will have a day bed and a small desk. The reader will be able to gaze over the rooftops towards central London, do

The kitchen and informal dining area opens out on to a small roof garden.

"The straw bale walls cost very little and were built in three and a half days by a group of friends and former students…"

A bridge at ▶ first floor separates the sleeping and living areas.

which is on rollers. Both are designed to accommodate the movement between the bedroom wing on solid ground and the living and work areas, which begin at first floor level and are sprung.

Despite all its intentional wackiness the house is highly practical. There is underfloor heating in the office area as well as the ground floor of the accommodation wing and a woodburning stove in the living room. Most of the walls to the south are glass, attracting much warmth into the building.

There is abundant natural light and ventilation: the polycarbonate roof to the two-storey entrance hall imports light that is redirected via the half-height walls in the kitchen and also the first floor bridge that separates the sleeping and main living areas. More light is brought into the

living area by the clerestory windows in the rear north elevation.

The walls on the north and west sides are made of straw bales. The 550 bales are not just piled on top of one another but enclosed within the timber studding that takes the floor and roof loads. They are capped with an overhanging eave of zinc to protect the vulnerable straw from the elements. On the outside there are some see-through panels of polycarbonate. The rest is covered with ribbed galvanised steel. "The straw bale walls cost very little and were built in three-and-a-half days by a group of friends and former students," says Sarah.

In many ways the house, with its rainwater recycling system that feeds the garden, office toilets and washing machine is a thorough and practical demonstration of how to redevelop an inner city brownfield site for a modern live/work environment largely using materials that are recycled, sustainable and involve a minimum of waste.

As well as the water recycling system the house incorporates a passive solar panel that heats domestic hot water ▶

The eastern elevation is dominated by sandbags covered by a fabric which Jeremy and Sarah hope will decay, leaving an imprint on the sand, lime and cement.

and a composting toilet in the main bedroom suite. This produces compost for the garden that is processed in a container in the undercroft. Eventually the two plan to grow their own vegetables.

The undercroft – effectively the ground floor of the house – is left largely open on the steel stilts which support the building. Here there remain some tell-tale clues to the small engineering works that stood on the site until 1998. Two underground tanks store 3,000 litres of rainwater from the office roof.

"Some have dubbed it the new 'stately home of Holloway…'"

As well as being likely to remain unfinished, the building has been left deliberately rough-at-the-edges in several places. It is tempting to say it is too full of ideas until the penny drops that over-the-top multiplicity is one of its main objects.

Some have dubbed it the new "stately home of Holloway." Less polite comments have included "a cliché-ridden, tongue-in-cheek spoof." One thing is certain – the house has invention tumbling out of every corner, and as one architectural critic comments: "Just be glad that someone built it".

If you wish to join one of the tours (there is a £3 fee) that take place from time to time you will find details on Sarah's website – www.swarch.co.uk. ■

FLOORPLAN: The house is very much designed to keep living and work separate, with the grand dining/conference hall as the link between the two.

Fact File costs as of Oct 2002

NAMES: Sarah Wigglesworth and Jeremy Till

PROFESSIONS: Architects

AREA: North London

HOUSE TYPE: Two bedroom live/work project

HOUSE SIZE: Living: 264m², office 210m²

BUILD ROUTE: Main contractor

CONSTRUCTION: Steel frame; variety of claddings

WARRANTY: None

SAP RATING: Not known

FINANCE: Ecology Building Society

BUILD TIME: 27 months

LAND COST: £78,000

BUILD COST: £300,000 plus £200,000 for office

TOTAL COST: £578,000

CURRENT VALUE: £1m

COST/m²: £1,055

42% COST SAVING

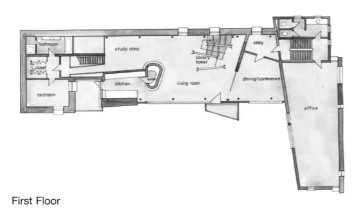

First Floor

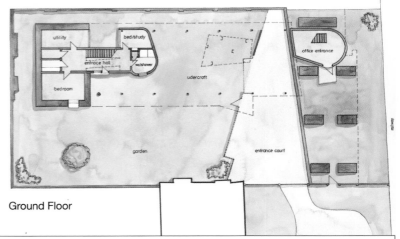

Ground Floor

USEFUL CONTACTS: Architects – Sarah Wigglesworth Architects: 020 7607 9200; **Structural engineers** – Price and Myers: 020 7631 5128; **Project managers and builders** – Koya Construction: 020 7639 6255; **Mechanical and electrical consultant** – Richard Pearce: 020 8429 8018; **Planning consultant** – Peter Kyte Associates: 020 8381 4311; **Lighting consultant** – Claudia Clements: 020 7240 4042; **Steelwork** – Joy Steel: 020 7474 0550; **Composting toilet** – Kingsley Clivus: 01837 83154; **Finance** – Ecology Building Society: 0845 674 5566; **Water consultants** – Elemental Solutions: 01594 516063; **Straw bale insulation** – Abbots: 01608 643675

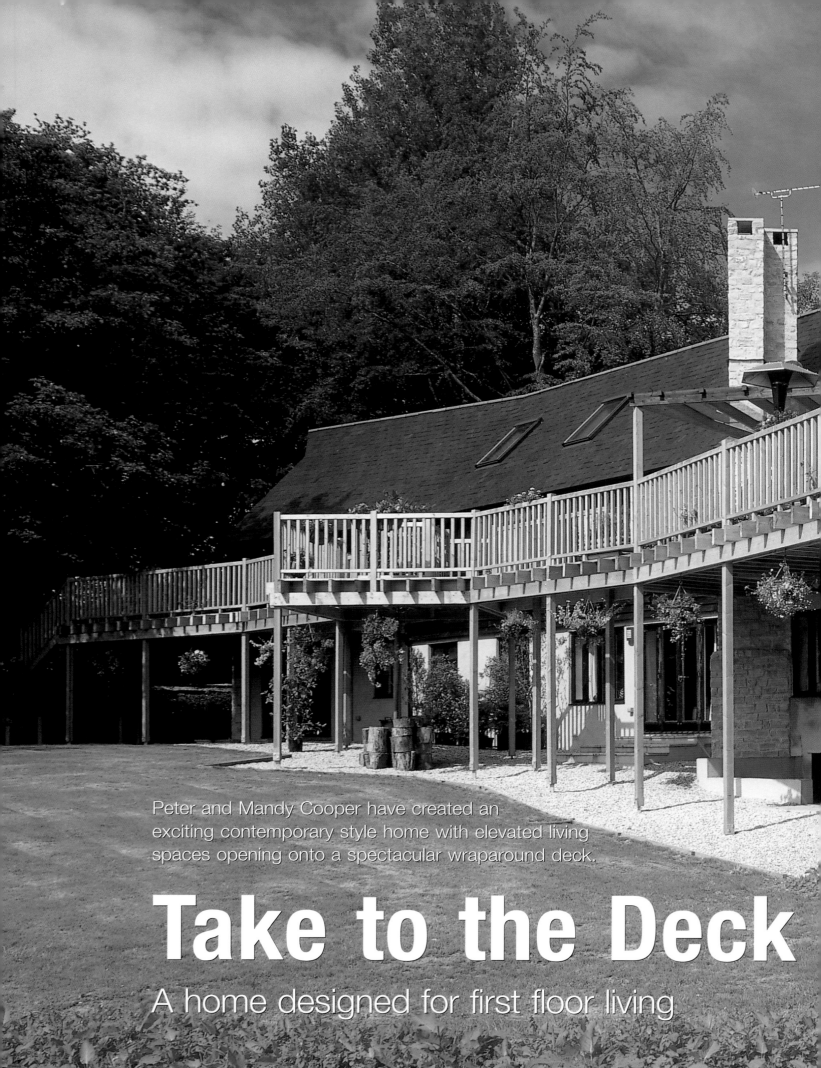

Peter and Mandy Cooper have created an exciting contemporary style home with elevated living spaces opening onto a spectacular wraparound deck.

Take to the Deck

A home designed for first floor living

Words:
Debbie Jeffery
Photography:
Nigel Rigden

With increasing numbers of people choosing to work from home, the concept of living and working in the same place is not unusual. When you are the directors of a residential field study centre for children, however, it is vital to be available outside of office hours. "Peter and I had been living in a village about 14 miles away from Hooke Court, travelling in to work each day," explains Mandy Cooper. "We needed to be available during the evenings and weekends, however, and were desperate for visitors' accommodation, an office area and a function room. The answer was to build a house which combined all of these elements."

Hooke Court is a 16th century, Grade II* listed manor house constructed in natural Ham stone, which caters for groups of children who visit West Dorset to experience the countryside whilst attending a range of practical educational programmes. Mandy and Peter began running the centre in 1994. "They were empty buildings looking for a use," says Mandy, a former headteacher. The main house had been used as a Church of England boarding school and offered ideal accommodation for a field study centre.

"Gaining planning permission for a new dwelling in the grounds of a listed building took quite some time," Peter Cooper recalls. "We approached a local architect and a planning consultant, who eventually secured outline planning permission for a home with offices below." The next step was to seek out an architect who could design a contemporary house which would complement both the Court and the woodland site in a corner of the grounds.

The couple contacted the Royal Institute of British Architects and were furnished with contacts for three RIBA ▶

The first floor ▶ living room is overlooked by a gallery walkway reached via a spiral staircase (ABOVE).

The kitchen/ ▶ breakfast room is located on the first floor and opens out onto the wraparound deck (BELOW) via French doors.

"Delays were commonplace and the six to eight month build time stretched to sixteen…"

The large ▶ floor to ceiling glazed screen and French windows ensure that the master bedroom on the ground floor is an extremely light room.

architects in the area. Phil Easton of Western Design, Dorset, had experience of working with listed buildings and offered design solutions which perfectly suited the Coopers' unusual requirements.

"We were determined not to build a square, boxy property," says Mandy. "Peter and I wanted something constructed using natural materials which would effectively divide work and living areas — preferably with our private accommodation on the first floor. We had previously owned a property with the sitting room upstairs leading out onto a large balcony, which we loved. Living at treetop height brings another dimension to a house."

The Coopers had spent a number of years in Africa, and hoped to bring some of their experiences to their new home. Phil Easton's imaginative solution is an unusual

south-facing design which won him the accolade for the best workspace in the Town and Country Design Awards, successfully combining public areas with a very private home inside the confines of one building. "We were especially impressed by the environment the architect had created for disabled people, with accommodation of a very high standard," commented the RIBA judges.

Principal rooms benefit from full height windows to take advantage of the woodland views, giving the impression of being high up in the tree canopy. The 440m^2 building has six bedrooms and a large balcony walkway, which wraps itself around the Purbeck stone and timber clad exterior, offering easy access to the outdoors.

Phil Easton has taken great care to avoid square rooms, introducing angular walls and windows throughout the building. The roof has been designed as a series of dramatic stepped shapes jutting out above the glass. "Our first floor living accommodation is completely separate from the rooms below," says Mandy. "We are totally unaware of noise or activity on the ground floor, as soundproofing was an important consideration at the design stage."

When it came to choosing a builder Mandy insisted on using a small, local firm who had previously tackled some minor works for the family. "I went against Phil Easton's advice and take full responsibility for what happened next," says Mandy. "Phil got quotes from a few contractors, but I wanted to support a small business. They just did not have the manpower or resources to tackle such a project, however, and it soon became apparent that all was not well."

Delays were commonplace and the six to eight month build time stretched to sixteen. Peter and Mandy rented out their house and moved into a campervan on site – eventually taking over the project management and subcontracting out work to various tradesmen. "We had never built before and it was a steep learning curve," says Mandy. "Every morning I tried to organise the few men who had turned up, purchased materials and chased orders."

To make matters worse the build itself was fraught with difficulties. Natural springs on the site necessitated the installation of French drains, the foundations filled with water and no-one seemed to know how best to lay the maple flooring which had been specified throughout the interiors. "The maple couldn't go down until the plastering was finished, but the plasterers needed a floor to stand on," laughs Peter. "Eventually we organised chipboard to be laid, but it took forever before the builders could agree on how the maple would be fixed into place. It was farcical, and we abandoned the wood downstairs and have used carpet and Indian slate over areas which have underfloor heating."

Changes to the original plans were made throughout the build. The Coopers noticed a large void beneath the office, due to a slight slope on the site, and decided to make use of this by incorporating an undercroft area ▶

A more formal reception room is located on the ground floor.

A viewing gallery has been built into the roofspace above the living areas with storage in the eaves.

Fact File costs as of Feb 2003

NAMES: Mandy and Peter Cooper

PROFESSIONS: School Directors

AREA: Dorset

HOUSE TYPE: Six bed home + office

HOUSE SIZE: 440m²

BUILD ROUTE: Builder and self-managed subbies

CONSTRUCTION: Blockwork and stone walls, timber cladding, slate roof

WARRANTY: Zurich Municipal

SAP RATING: 83

FINANCE: Lloyds

BUILD TIME: 16 months

LAND COST: already owned

BUILD COST: £340,000

TOTAL COST: £340,000

HOUSE VALUE: £600,000

43% COST SAVING

COST/m²: £773

Cost Breakdown:

Planning and fees	£27,000
Build costs	£245,000
Service connections and installations	£34,000
Tiles and tiling	£9,500
Kitchen and bathroom	£17,000
Landscaping/clearane	£7,500
TOTAL	**£340,000**

First Floor

[Floor plan labels: dress, bath, master bedroom, bed, bed, living room, wc, utility, kitchen, sun deck, sun deck]

Ground Floor

[Floor plan labels: utility, store, bath, kitchen, wc, guest lounge/diner, guest bed, guest bed, office, office, reception room]

which offers useful storage space. They also chose to open up the gallery above their living rooms. "A walkway was planned to extend halfway across the kitchen, with the remaining roof space used as an attic," explains Peter. "During the build we questioned why we were enclosing such a wonderful space, and decided to leave the entire area open to the roof, retaining storage in the eaves."

In addition to managing the build the Coopers tackled a large amount of the physical work themselves, particularly during the final six months — when they roped in friends and relatives to help with carpentry, decorating and landscaping and even organised family painting weekends! When it came to finding fittings the couple finally had some luck.

"We wanted contemporary pieces which would complement the design," says Peter. "Mandy and I wandered into a shop and discovered that they were just about to change their display items, which they agreed to sell at a knock-down price! Three bathrooms and the kitchen were fitted out to a very high standard in this way."

In August the builders took a two week holiday and Mandy decided that, while she had the opportunity, she would take a break and travel to South Africa with her daughter to purchase furniture. "I wanted chunky modern items in wood and leather, but to commission them in this country would have cost a fortune," she states. "We found a furniture designer with a small factory and purchased a combination of standard designs and purpose-made pieces to fit individual spaces. Even the huge table legs have been carved to match a mirror in the reception room downstairs."

The building effectively turns its back on Hooke Court, with all major windows looking south across the surrounding fields, so that when Peter and Mandy sit on their deck they are not overlooking their place of work. "Living and working in the same building has its benefits — we don't need to spend time commuting, for example," says Peter. "This house has met all of our requirements. It echoes the surrounding buildings but is modern and innovative in design. We couldn't be more pleased." ∎

FLOORPLAN: The house has been designed with a long plan so that all principal rooms may face south towards the sun and country views. Living accommodation is at first floor level, with offices, visitors' accommodation and reception rooms beneath.

USEFUL CONTACTS: **Architect** - Western Design: 01258 455239; **Balcony** - Millennium Carpenters: 01308 423203; **Maple flooring** - Peter Newman: 01202 747175; **Tiles** - Terra Firma: 01264 810315; **Balustrade** - Spindlewood: 01278 453665; **Stone and Polished Hearths** - Landers Quarries: 01929 439205; **Plumbing** - Chris Rampton, Dorchester: 01305 848384; **Electrics** - Delve Electrical: 01404 42958; **Kitchen and Bathrooms fittings** - Avery Interiors: 01494 730200; **Staircases** - Monk Woodworking: 01935 425232; **Furniture and Crafts** – colonialinteriors@mail.com

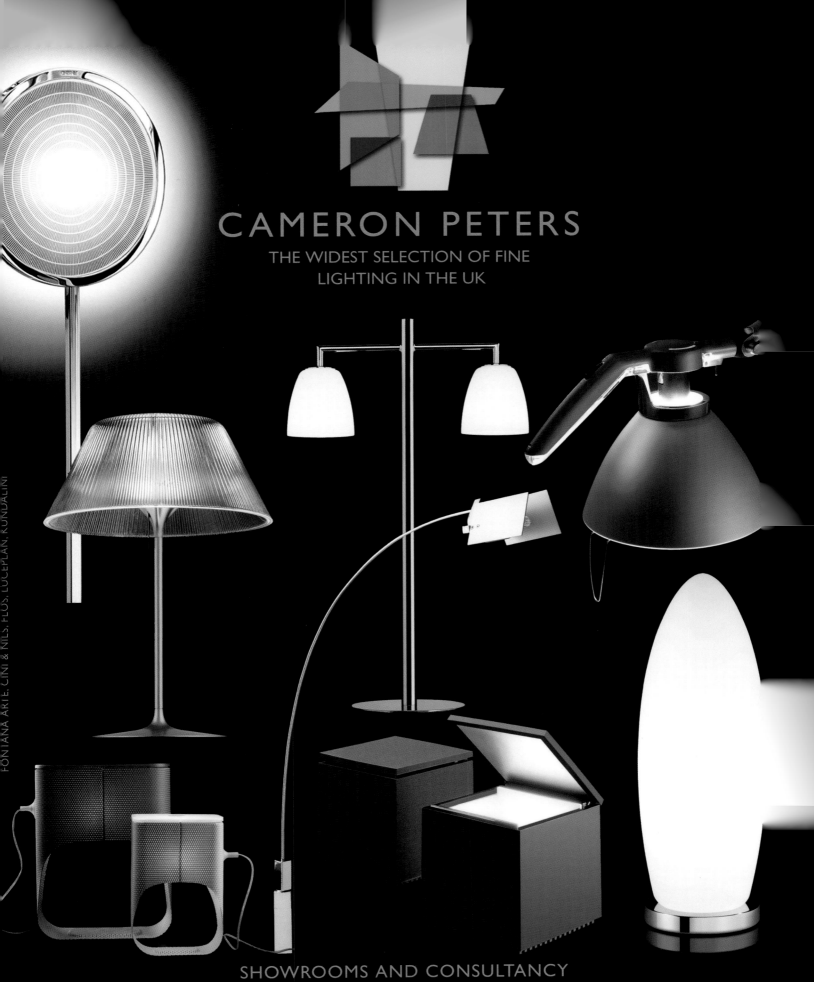

CAMERON PETERS

THE WIDEST SELECTION OF FINE
LIGHTING IN THE UK

FONTANA ARTE, CINI & NILS, FLOS, LUCEPLAN, KUNDALINI

SHOWROOMS AND CONSULTANCY
THE OLD DAIRY, HOME FARM, ARDINGTON, WANTAGE OX12 8PD
Tel: 01235 835 000 WWW.CAMERONPETERS.CO.UK

Jacob's Ladder has been built on the footprint of a dilapidated house which was constructed by the Dean of Windsor for his family.

Down

Architectural experiment or practical
modern house? Whatever your view,
David and Shelley Grey's new self-built
home certainly gives visitors to its
hideaway location a surprise.

Words: **Debbie Jeffery**   Photography: **David Grey**

In The Woods

Without exception everyone who visits Jacob's Ladder, nestled in its woodland setting, is in awe of this fantastic modern structure. Building the house proved far from easy, however, and its owners, David and Shelley Grey, are only now beginning to relax after the stressful process. "We never set out to own an award-winning house," laughs David, "and, although we find it incredible to live in, we were rather naive when it came to the build process itself."

Their project started when, becoming concerned about the increasing traffic passing outside their previous home – a beautiful Georgian vicarage — the couple decided to self-build. "We loved the house but, after five years, knew it was time to move on," says Shelley. "It had become almost impossible to sit out in the garden due to the noise from the traffic, and we decided that what we needed was space."

Nine and a half acres of private beech woodland is about as much space as any two people could require and, when a chance comment from a friend led to the Greys viewing the plot, they knew they had found the answer. Complete with a derelict 1950s house and full planning ▶

The double height living room is overlooked by the master bedroom above.

Views from the first floor entrance deck out over the internal pool and flooded swimming pool roof to the west.

"For a long time we had thought it would be quite good fun to build a house — although 'fun' isn't a word I'd use any more!"

permission for a traditional replacement dwelling, the woods offered a peace and privacy most of us can only dream of. "For a long time we had thought it would be quite good fun to build a house — although 'fun' isn't a word I'd use any more!" says David.

A sealed bid won them the site, which is within a conservation area, and the option to build the "heavy-looking" property the planners had approved. "What the woodland needed was a light house, which acknowledged its surroundings rather than dominating them," says Shelley. "We looked through The Architecture Foundation's *New Architects* book and approached twelve practices. Niall McLaughlin Architects was number thirteen."

David spent a great deal of time visiting the various architects, but found it extraordinary that only two actually wanted to come to the site. "When Niall walked into the room we had instant rapport. The question that we asked ourselves was: 'would we trust this man with all our worldly wealth?' Niall has a lot of gravitas and credibility. He brought a pile of books and we sat on the floor showing him the things that we liked — it was very exciting to see ideas evolving."

Although they admit that their knowledge of architecture and design was minimal, when the Greys picked out houses by the likes of Mies van der Rohe and Corbusier, Niall knew that the house would be drawn from early Modernist essays. He began with the Tugendhat villa, built by Mies van der Rohe in Czechoslovakia — which has a strong visual relationship with the landscape, distinct ▶

Genvex

Heat Recovery Ventilation and Air/Water Heat Pumps

Breathing life into today's homes

- Recovers as much as 95% of the heat from the extracted air

- Eliminates condensation problems

- Lowers the risk of allergy and asthma by reducing house mites to a minimum

- Genvex Heat Pumps can provide up to 80% of annual heating requirements.

- Provides comfort cooling in the summer

- Less traffic noise and added security, as windows can remain closed year round

- Lowers the concentration of organic solvents from building materials and household goods

- Reduces radon radiation from the ground

- Genvex Heat Pumps can provide up to 80% of annual heating requirements

- Comfort cooling in summer

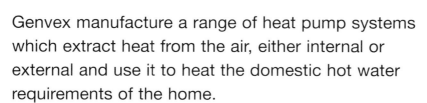

Domestic water heating pump

Vanvex 185/190 and 290/295 domestic water heating pumps utilise the heat from the home and from the outside air to heat domestic water.

- Supplies hot water all year round

- Energy saving at least equal to that provided by solar heating

- Energy conserving system

- Capacity of up to respectively 325 (Vanvex 185/190) and 425 (Vanvex 290/295) litres of hot water per 24 hours (60 degrees Celsius)

- Internal enamel surface in the hot water tank provides protection against corrosion

- External capacitor

- The price for heating domestic water is approximately 1/3 of the price relative to an electric water heater

- Reduces the concentration of organic solvents from building materials and furniture

- Built-in electrical heating element (1 kW)

- The tank can be used as a buffer tank for oil-fired or gas-fired central heating during the winter with the help of a coil in the tank (maximum temperature 60 degrees Celsius) only Vanvex 290

Genvex manufacture a range of heat pump systems which extract heat from the air, either internal or external and use it to heat the domestic hot water requirements of the home.

Combi-S can be used in homes with areas of between 80 and 120m^2, minimum air replacement: 120m^3/h. Combi-XL can be used in homes with areas of between 120-170m^2. Minimum air replacement: 160m^3/h. Both models are capable of covering a family's hot water needs and partially covering the basic heating of the ventilation air.

Teknik HRV Ltd
PO Box 199
Hereford HR1 1YN

Tel: 01432 376911 Fax: 01432 376912

Email: genvex.is4d@btopenworld.com

▲ The timber staircase is enclosed within an opaque glass wall, inspired by the Tugendhat villa built by Mies van der Rohe in Czechoslovakia.

areas of accommodation linked by a flat roof, and a curved glass wall around the inner stairs.

"David and Shelley gave me a wonderful brief," recalls Niall, who was selected as the Young Architect of the Year in 1998. "Coming from a compartmentalised Georgian house, where they only ate in the dining room four times in five years, they wanted a more open building — with rooms that could be used even when they were empty." His partially open plan response frames the views, with glazing on all sides and internal windows ensuring that several areas of the house may be seen at once. A single storey swimming pool wing, with glass walls, shoots off from the simple rectangle of the main structure to create an eye-catching feature.

Although the local planning officer preferred the concept of a traditional house, with a pitched tiled roof, she accepted that the new property would not be overlooked in any way — permitting an altogether more contemporary glazed steel framed design.

"I told Niall that the two ways of getting himself fired would be to give us a red pitched tiled roof or a blue swimming pool!" laughs David.

The nature of the setting ensures total privacy, which made the concept of a glass house a practical consideration. "We have no curtains in the house at all — even in the bathroom," says Shelley. "Our driveway is 200 metres long, with an electric entrance gate and CCTV security cameras — so we don't worry about unexpected guests dropping by!"

"I still get a buzz every time I come home... it really is the most fantastic place to live."

Work began on site in January 2000, with a completion date scheduled for nine months later. Concrete pads support the structural steel frame, which was erected in under two days and then clad in glass and warm coloured Douglas fir. After a year had passed the Greys grew concerned that something was amiss, and their fears were confirmed when the builder's company went into liquidation – leaving the building unfinished.

"I actually gave up work for a year to protect our investment and complete the house, whilst we continued living in rented accommodation," says David. "It wasn't what we had planned, and various other people let us down so that a lot of the work needed to be redone at our expense. It was far more difficult than we had expected, but we soon took off our rose-tinted spectacles."

One piece of advice concerns the builder's insurance. "We found out that our contractor was under-insured for our project – which meant that the insurance company would only pay a percentage of our losses," he says.

Living in a woodland setting brings its own benefits and ensures that the log fire is always well stocked. Additionally, underfloor heating has been laid throughout the building, with trench heaters sited beneath ground floor windows to prevent condensation. David cut his own beech trees from around the house, which were kiln dried and machined to create floorboards for the interiors, and wild cherry trees were also felled – some of which have been used to build a wood and steel framed dining table.

With the house completed after almost two years the Greys have finally moved in. Jacob's Ladder, which received an RIBA 2002 Award, is perched on the steeply sloping hillside, with its glass walls built close to the surrounding beech trees. Niall McLaughlin designed a single gap in the dense enclosure of trees which gives a view into the valley below.

Water plays an important part in the design, with the black tiled exercise pool actually giving you the impression of swimming out into the landscape. The silver ceiling of the pool house reflects the light, and Shelley suggested that this wing should have a flooded roof – which adds a further glassy, reflective element to this extraordinary new house.

"I still get a buzz every time I come home," David Grey remarks. "You arrive through the woodland and are greeted by the back of the house – which appears very strange. A gangplank bridge leads onto the first floor entrance deck and from here there are views out over the internal pool and flooded swimming pool roof to the west. It really is the most fantastic place to live." ■

Fact File costs as of Dec 2002

NAMES: David and Shelley Grey

PROFESSIONS: Photographer/Film Director and Lawyer

AREA: West Country

HOUSE TYPE: Detached contemporary

HOUSE SIZE: 260m²

BUILD ROUTE: Contractor and subcontractor

CONSTRUCTION: Steel frame clad in glass and Douglas fir

BUILD TIME: Jan '00 – Dec '01

LAND COST: £250,000

BUILD COST: £412,000

TOTAL COST: £662,000

HOUSE VALUE: £1 million+

COST/m²: £1,585

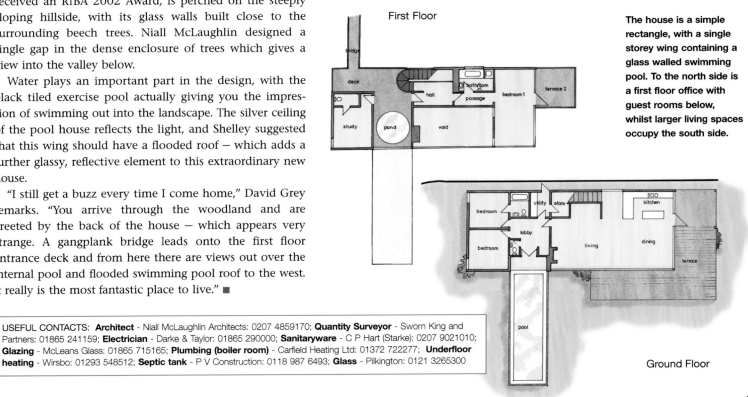

First Floor

Ground Floor

The house is a simple rectangle, with a single storey wing containing a glass walled swimming pool. To the north side is a first floor office with guest rooms below, whilst larger living spaces occupy the south side.

USEFUL CONTACTS: **Architect** - Niall McLaughlin Architects: 0207 4859170; **Quantity Surveyor** - Sworn King and Partners: 01865 241159; **Electrician** - Darke & Taylor: 01865 290000; **Sanitaryware** - C P Hart (Starke): 0207 9021010; **Glazing** - McLeans Glass: 01865 715165; **Plumbing (boiler room)** - Carfield Heating Ltd: 01372 722277; **Underfloor heating** - Wirsbo: 01293 548512; **Septic tank** - P V Construction: 0118 987 6493; **Glass** - Pilkington: 0121 3265300

Replacing a suburban dwelling with a modernist home

Back to the Future

The design of John and Heather Hunter's spacious new home in Kent was strongly influenced by the 1930s International Modernist movement.

W hen you consider the dramatic depth of the double height spaces and the extraordinary four metre high front door, it is not surprising that John and Heather Hunter decided to call their stylish contemporary new home in Orpington, Kent, 'High Planes'.

You don't fully absorb the individuality of the Hunters' new home, however, until you compare it to its predominantly Tudorbethan neighbours in this edge of Green Belt suburb. A real target for teardown development, several houses have already been demolished and replaced with sizeable suburban homes of the style immortally categorised as 'Bank Manager Baroque.' Infilling has added to the predictably comfortable and well maintained but visually unchallenging area.

The Hunters appear to be a conventional enough couple — a retired accountant and his textile designer wife; quite at home, one would think, both in the area and its style of housing. So how did they come to be building such a different type of house? How did they get away with it from a planning point of view? And how did they carry it out? ▶

Words:
Jude Webley

Photography:
Philip Bier

The narrow ▶ hallway is 4m high. The door to the right leads to a staircase down to the basement level.

"Over the course of a year or so we realised we just were not going to find the right place…"

The Hunters lived and worked near Chicago for a number of years prior to retirement. "We've always been interested in modern art and architecture but while we were in the States we had the opportunity to visit most of Frank Lloyd Wright's houses," explains John.

"If you want to see exciting towers and urban landscapes, Chicago is the place. Looking around at the sort of houses that are available over there is a real eye-opener. We became used to the light and space you get in modern American homes and so were aware that there are alternatives to the conventional British suburban home.

"When we returned to the UK we lived in our family home which we had rented out while we were away but we felt dissatisfied with it and decided to try and find a house that suited us better. We wanted to stay within this particular area and over the course of a year or so we realised we just were not going to find the right place. So we decided to get started trying to build one."

A search for a plot and an architect were both eventually successful. The 'plot' was in fact a Scandinavian style timber frame house that had been built in the 1970s and which sat on a decent sized plot with a back garden that included natural woodland. The house, which would be

The stair fits ▶ into the overlap between the two rectangular spaces that form the basis of the design and leads to the small bridge which links the different areas.

demolished, cost £260,000 in 1998. "There were no plots available so we were forced to buy a house to knock down. It's a rather expensive way of buying a plot and it certainly added cost to the project as a whole," says John.

RIBA's Client Advisory Service put the Hunters in touch with seven architectural practices who had done work of the type they were interested in. Having seen their portfolios they interviewed two and went to look at some examples of their work. John and Heather particularly liked a flat conversion they went to see in Notting Hill designed by AEM and so decided to work with them despite the fact that the practice had never built a new home for a client before.

The Hunters set about explaining their wish list and budget to the architects. They wanted to build a modern but not a minimalist house. They wanted a substantial master bedroom suite plus another two bedrooms separately located; a music room off the main living space; a study area and a studio. But principally they wanted a huge open plan living area with big windows and lots of light.

"They were incredibly business-like clients," recalls Pascal Maddocks-Jones of AEM. "We started coming up with plans and sketches which the Hunters would study and then critique with us when we met. They'd really think about the proposals and they got to be really tuned in to the design process. I'd say it was one of the most creative relationships we've had with private clients."

John and Heather enjoyed this process too: "The relationship with Pascal was like a dance," explains Heather. "He had a subtle way of letting us know that he had a new idea for us. The design gradually evolved."

Now the architect had to sell the concept to the planners. The notion of rebuilding a similar style dwelling is not normally contested by the planners. But what was being proposed was in no way similar either to the original house or to anything else in the neighbourhood, ▶

Useful Contacts

Architect — AEM:	0207 713 9191
RIBA Client Advisory Service:	www.architecture.com
Structural Engineer — Elliot Wood Partnership:	
	0208 544 0033
Quantity Surveyor — Stockdales:	0208 664 6373
Main Contractor — Franklin Building:	01245 505050
Roof (Corrugated Cementitious Sheets) — Eternit:	
	01763 264600
Walls — Durox solid block:	01375 644244
Underfloor Heating — Wirsbo:	01293 548512
Garage Door — Hormann:	01530 513000
Patio Doors — Rainham Fabrications:	020 8592 2589
Showers — Grohe:	020 8594 7292

John and Heather have decided not to bother with a separate dining room at all, incorporating it into the living space.

which was part of a private estate and subject to certain covenants which had been designed to safeguard the interests of the residents.

"The planners at Bromley took quite a relaxed view," explains the architect, "on the basis that the plot was not in a Conservation Area. If we could convince the neighbours and the Residents' Association Planning Sub-committee, the planners would be happy. To start with there was a lot of noise but we were lucky to have an architect on the Committee who gradually convinced the others that the scheme had merit."

In the end the Residents' Association rejected the final development proposal but the immediate neighbours were happy and lodged no objections. Detailed consent was ▶

Fact File costs as of Feb 2002

NAME: John and Heather Hunter	**SAP RATING:** Not known
PROFESSION: Retired Accountant and Fabric Designer	**FINANCE:** Private
	BUILD TIME: Jan '99 — Dec '99
AREA: Kent	**LAND COST:** £260,000
HOUSE TYPE: Contemporary	**BUILD COST:** £402,000
HOUSE SIZE: 268m²	**TOTAL COST:** £662,000
BUILD ROUTE: Architect & contractor	**HOUSE VALUE:** £800,000
CONSTRUCTION: Solid lightweight block and steel	**COST/M²:** £1,500

17% COST SAVING

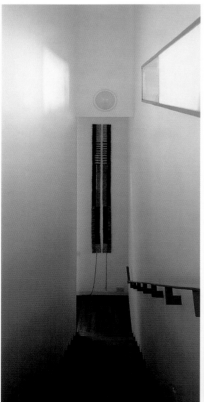

"We were also impressed that it was completed on time and that there were very few problems on the snagging list…"

▲ The large glazed section on the rear, south facing elevation could cause overheating within the dwelling and so the couple have included an electronically operated awning to provide shade.

FLOORPLAN: The house is notionally designed in two volumes, with the sleeping areas in one rectangular block and the living areas in another, linked by a bridge at first floor level. A curved wall helps to demarcate the work and relaxation areas on both levels. There is also a full basement level which is used for storage.

First Floor

bedroom 1

void

studio

study

void

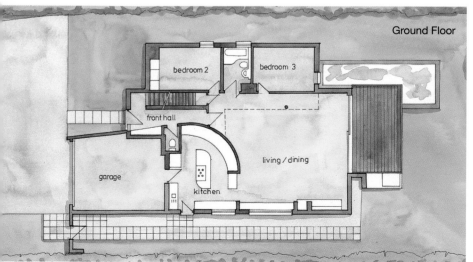

Ground Floor

bedroom 2

bedroom 3

front hall

garage

kitchen

living / dining

obtained without ever meeting the planners. The only lobbying was to the local community who, in effect, decided the outcome.

So all systems were go. The project was put out to tender by the architect. The late decision to add a full basement altered the budget significantly but having lived in America where everyone has a basement this made sense. A lot of storage space in an open style house of this sort is essential in reducing clutter.

"The budget figures did alter during the discussions with the architect," explains John. "But once we had decided what we wanted, Pascal used a quantity surveyor to assess the likely cost and that figure was very accurate. The contract came in within 3% of the quotation, all based on slight alterations which were agreed with us beforehand. We were also impressed that it was completed on time and that there were very few problems on the snagging list."

"I'd encourage anyone interested in contemporary design to pursue their dream. It's worth it."

At £1,500/m² this project is at the top end of the cost scale. Building genuine one-offs of this sort does not come cheap and the fact that there is such a large double height area reduces the available floor area dramatically and hence the apparent cost per metre.

Technically the house has a few innovations. It is built of solid lightweight blockwork with no cavity wall. "This is the sensible way to build as far as I'm concerned," explains the architect, "as in my opinion cavity walls just lead to problems. Either the builders leave muck in the cavity which can lead to moisture penetrating across to the inner leaf or you get problems with the detailing of the cavity trays around the doors and windows. A solid block gives excellent thermal performance and is relatively simple to build, even more so now that you can do it with a thin mortar joint." All the floors use pre-cast concrete 'planks' which helps improve acoustic insulation and creates an excellent base for the underfloor heating.

"We're really pleased with the house, which is a lovely place to live in," concludes John. "We've now got the space and light we were keen to have and the good thing is that it works as a place to live. We'd thought long and hard about living in a place with such high ceilings worrying that it might be oppressive. During the project planning stage we visited lots of art galleries and other public buildings with high volume spaces to try and judge whether we would like living in that kind of environment. Fortunately it's turned out that we do. I'd encourage anyone interested in contemporary design to pursue their dream. It's worth it." ■

Uponor - The Smarter choice for all Plumbing and Underfloor Heating installations.

- Warm friendly floors
- Flexible plastic piping
- Long lasting pre-insulated piping

Contact us to see how Uponor can provide the smarter choice

Uponor Housing Solutions Ltd
Snapethorpe House, Rugby Road, Lutterworth, Leicestershire, LE17 4HN
T: 01455 550355   F: 01455 550366   E: hsenquiries@uponor.co.uk   W: www.uponorhousingsolutions.co.uk

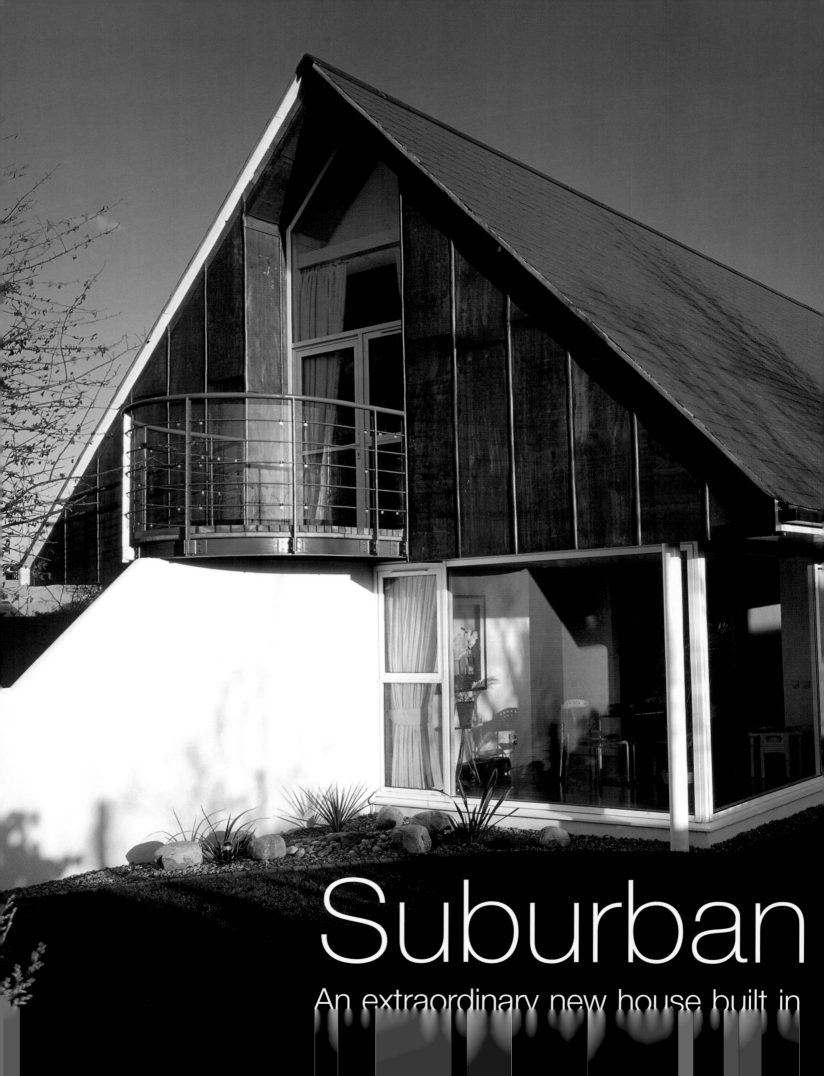

Suburban

An extraordinary new house built in

Chic
an ordinary setting

James and Hayley Keates have created an exciting modern family home with elegant living spaces on an infill garden plot in an ordinary suburban setting.

D oes a family home have to follow the traditional mould? Not according to James and Hayley Keates, who in their late twenties have built a successful contemporary home that blends in happily with the leafy suburbs of an everyday Staffordshire town.

Their home is more than a piece of stylish London Loft minimalism. It has bags of atmosphere and combines open plan living with a successful function as a real home for two young professionals and their two very young children. There cannot be too many young parents who would not be pretty pleased to have built themselves a home of this style and quality. All the more amazing considering it is their first home.

How did they manage it? James and Hayley are the first to acknowledge that they had a pretty good start. Hayley's father is an architect (Roy Manning of Eaton, Manning and Wilson). Keen on contemporary design, he worked with the couple designing this home and donated his services for free. If that was not enough of a bonus, they were able to continue their full time jobs as James's father, Laurence, a retired Planning Officer, volunteered to act as Site Agent and co-ordinate all the subcontractors and the ordering and delivery of materials.

"We were happy to take all the advantages we could get," smiles Hayley with no trace of embarrassment. "I've always lived in modern houses and wanted to carry on when I left home," she says. "We were both living at home with our parents but when we got engaged we started looking for an existing house with the intention of changing it. The trouble is you have to pay a lot for the original house and then a lot more to turn it into the house you want."

Words:
Jude Webley

Photography:
Mark Welsh

►

123

"We were keen that the garden, which would be very visible… would be treated almost as an extra room…"

The front door ▲ leads to a hallway and on into a double height dining area with a huge glazed section overlooking the gardens.

Roy heard of a suburban infill plot about to come on to the market and the couple decided to pull out of buying a house they were pursuing and offer the asking price of £50,000, which was accepted. The plot had outline planning consent for a dormer bungalow. Roy then set about his task. His conception of what a dormer bungalow might look like is certainly challenging.

"We gave Roy a free hand at the design," explains James. "We said that we wanted a spacious open plan layout, plenty of glass and high ceilings in the upstairs rooms. We wanted the walls to be white internally and externally – to link inside and out – and we were keen that the garden, which would be very visible from the house due to the large amount of glazing, would be treated almost as an extra room of the house. Roy got something down on paper which we had a look at. We decided against the spiral staircase for safety reasons as we were intending to have kids and we changed some of the windows but we liked Roy's ideas."

Amazingly, planning sailed through as there were no objections to the scheme but on site things were destined to go more true to form. Since they were building a large house to a budget and had the free services of a project manager, it made sense to use subcontractors. Both families had a good range of builder contacts and spent time going to visit reference projects before deciding on ▶

A fabricated steel staircase fitted with beech laminate treads and risers leads to the first floor from the dining area. Shadowline mouldings in place of skirting and architrave, and internal doors which go all the way to the ceiling add cost but contribute to the atmosphere.

"We really suffered from the contractors disappearing to other jobs in the middle of our own..."

At the far end ▲ of the dining area is the main reception area, a generous and elegant space with floor to ceiling windows on two walls.

who to work with. "We worked mainly with people on a fixed price package of work," explains James, "and definitely found that this was an easier way of going about things than paying people on a day rate."

The main difficulty was not so much technical as to do with the perennial problem of keeping the men on site. "We really suffered from the contractors disappearing to other jobs in the middle of our own," recalls James. "Since we were originally in a rented house and latterly living rent free in the home of a departed grandparent, we weren't in a huge hurry to move in. But things did drag on and getting the project completed was difficult. My father came to the site every day and looked after ordering materials, co-ordinating the activities of the different contractors and pretty much everything else. We couldn't have done it without him!" Roy also kept an eye on things in his role as inspecting architect, issuing architect's certificates at the usual stages.

James and Hayley have clearly been blessed with extreme good fortune and there is plenty about this tale ▶

Useful Contacts

Architect —
Eaton, Manning, Wilson & Assoc:
01782 711822

Low-e Glazing — Pilkington K Glass:
01744 28882

Wooden Flooring — Junckers:
01376 517512

UFH — Wirsbo:
01293 548512

Reconstituted Rooftiles —
Marley-Eternit: 01675 468400

Garage Door — Crawfords:
01782 599899

Sanitaryware — Ideal Standard:
01482 346461

Aluminium Powder Coated Windows and Doors — Quality Glass:
01782 289700

Stairs (glass balustrade) — Quality Glass: 01782 289700

Stairs (timber treads) — Lancaster & Tomkinson: 01782 614156

Stairs (steelwork) — Reynolds & Litchfield: 01782 319029

Junkers Beech flooring is used throughout the ground floor. The Keates opted for a warm water underfloor heating system from Wirsbo which has proved very successful.

that sounds rather sugar coated. The lack of struggle will not ring true with many self-builders. They have ended up with a fabulous house and all the family relationships appear to still be intact. One disagreement between architect and 'client' involved James' and Hayley's insistence that they wanted to have Velux rooflights in their bedroom to increase the natural light and give views of the garden. The architect did not want the purity of his roofline spoiled. "It was a difficult dinner," sums up James succinctly.

Design purity also had to meet cost reality in a number of areas. Large spans of clear unsupported patent glazing were switched for a cheaper alternative. Stainless steel sockets and switches were substituted by plastic. Designer bathroom fittings will have to come later. "You've got to get the best quality design at a price you can afford," concludes James. ■

Low ▶ maintenance, powder coated aluminium doors and windows were used, fitted with energy efficient Pilkington K Glass.

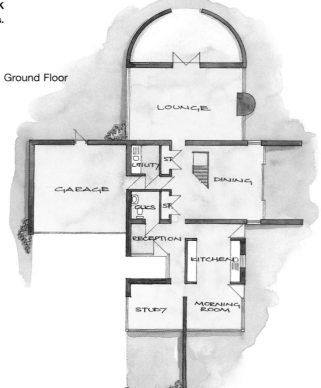

Ground Floor

First Floor

Fact File costs as of Aug 2001

NAMES: James and Hayley Keates

PROFESSION: Solicitor and teacher

AREA: Staffordshire

HOUSE TYPE: Contemporary

HOUSE SIZE: 310m^2 + 36m^2 garage

BUILD ROUTE: Local subcontractors managed by parents

CONSTRUCTION: Masonry with rendered blockwork

WARRANTY: Architect's Certificates

FINANCE: Staffordshire BS

BUILD TIME: May '96 — Mar '00

LAND COST: £50,000

BUILD COST: £176,500

TOTAL COST: £226,500

HOUSE VALUE: £300,000

COST/M^2: £509

25%
COST SAVING

Cost Breakdown:

Groundworks	£27,000
Superstructure	£57,000
Roof	£38,000
Heating & plumbing	£8,500
Lighting & electrical	£10,000
Plastering	£7,000
Finishes	£9,000
Kitchen & bathrooms	£15,000
Landscaping	£5,000
TOTAL	**£176,500**

Alan and Joan Cowell built a contemporary home in a stunning location using traditional techniques.

Words:
Clive Fewins

Photography:
Nigel Rigden

Alan Cowell was sitting in the departure lounge of Dublin Airport waiting for a flight to Manchester when he suddenly realised how struck he was with the design of the building. It was a hexagon with an open cathedral ceiling and it set him thinking about the design of the new house he was planning to build in South Wales with his wife Joan.

They had read H&R for several years during the planning stage of the project, which was spent in their overcrowded converted cowshed home on the outskirts of Cardiff.

"It was the usual story — we just couldn't find a barn to convert that was in the right position at the right price and the right size," says Alan, who is a headteacher in Cardiff, 25 miles from the village where their new house is situated. "We were also keen for my 75 year old widowed father Cyril to join us."

Eventually they heard of part of a former hill farm on the side of a steep valley near Port Talbot that was for sale. They immediately fell for the site. Alan loved the abundance of trees and Joan the fast flowing stream at the foot of what is now the garden.

"There were just six plots and four had been taken," says Alan. "I think this one had been rejected because of its long thin shape and because it was on the side of a valley, which would increase the price of the build. But it was just what we wanted.

The

▶

Hexagon House

Creating a modern oak frame home

The Hexagon House

▲ From the kitchen and breakfast area at the front of the building there are uninterrupted views right through the living areas and out over the valley and stream to the rear.

Waist-high glass partitions, ▶ framed in oak (RIGHT) act as balustrading between the different levels without obscuring the sightlines.

"Rather cheekily I offered the farmer £45,000 for the remaining two plots, totalling about 0.8 of an acre, the idea being to combine them and build a long low house that stepped down the valleyside. They had been on the market for £35,000 each. To my surprise he accepted."

Thanks to their moment of inspiration in the airport, by the time the Cowells approached architect John Thompson they had very definite ideas for the building. It was to be three hexagons – one of them the garage – and the framework for all the above ground living areas was to be of green oak.

▶

The generously ▶
proportioned
kitchen is from
Leekes of
Llantrisant.

▼ The oak
framed windows
were made by
Design Spec
(01275 845685).

Another key to the house was that it was to conform to the main Japanese tenet – the Cowells are great admirers of Japanese culture and architecture – of being asymmetrical. "There is hardly a room in new house that is in any sense a conventional rectangle or cube," says Alan.

Even the cavernous basement on the lower ground floor of the £400,000 house – built into the slope of a valley – is a highly irregular shape. On top of this massive basement, which also houses two en suite bedrooms, is a remarkable hexagon produced by Rupert Newman and his

"We did not specifically want to be eco, or to make money…"

team at Westwind Oak Buildings. Rupert was introduced to the Cowells, as was architect John Thompson of Bristol-based Barlow Henley, by Frameworks, a design and build consultancy specialising in oak framed buildings that they discovered through an advertisement in H&R.

The bathroom is modern in style with some Japanese influences.

"The house cost us around £400,000 to build and has showed us little profit so far… but we feel it is worth every penny."

▲ The flexibility of oak frame construction meant that, when the Cowells realised that their bedroom layout left them with no view from their bedroom, they were able to adapt it with little difficulty.

"We did not specifically want to be eco, or to make money: just to have a house with masses of timber in it and with as much Japanese influence as possible," says Joan who was very keen on being able to see the entire structure – barn-style – from within and to have soaring cathedral ceilings as a major element of the design.

They have managed to combine all these ideas into a remarkable house which also incorporates an asymmetrical exterior as well as the huge flowing two storey internal spaces they wanted so much. It is also a house with a 'wow factor.' As soon as you enter through the double oak and glass front doors into the porch you have no idea what is in store when you open the door the other side of the vestibule. In front of you oak roof timbers seem to be flying everywhere. The main structure is built around a gigantic chimney stack in local stone. The staircase winds round this – to the one bedroom upstairs and the two en suite guest rooms below.

On the ground floor the house makes the most of the sloping site. Four steps in black slate lead from the higher kitchen/diner level to the main living room area that focuses on the open fire in the central hearth. The downstairs floors are of maple strip, while upstairs in the main en suite bedroom the floor is of western red pine. This room has a complete view of the soaring downstairs living room through a shoji, a transparent sliding Japanese screen made from a form of rice paper.

The second hexagonal living area is occupied by Cyril. This is not such a clearly defined hexagon as the main living area because the walls on the far side – the north-east – have been 'cut away' to form Cyril's bathroom and adjoining bedroom.

There is no upstairs in this section of the house. The room that serves as Cyril's sitting room and dining room is dominated by a huge hexagonal oak post that supports the roof. The ceiling, like that of the main hexagon, is boarded and painted, this time white.

Between these two hexagons the glass conservatory at the south west facing rear is an integral part of the building. Inside the spaces flow into one another without the use of internal walls. From the kitchen and breakfast area at the front of the building there are uninterrupted views right through the living areas and out over the ▶

USEFUL CONTACTS: **Architects** - Barlow Henley: 0117 944 1777; **Structural engineers** – Structural Solutions: 0117 944 5556; **Oak frame** - West Wind: 01934 877317; **Groundworks** - Port Talbot Labour and Plant: 01639 883333; **Frameworks design and build consultancy**: 01934 733536; **Windows** - Design Spec: 01275 845685; **Heating and plumbing** - Andy Llewellyn: 01291 621634; **Underfloor heating** - Rettig: 01299 250700; **Stone** - R P Williams-Jones: 01656 862214; **Timber** - Timber Supplies: 0117 9691356; **Internal slate and marble** - Bullens: 01495 751720; **Kitchen** - Leekes of Llantrisant: 01443 667350

The staircase connecting the bedrooms winds round the central chimney which is built in local stone.

valley and stream to the rear. Balustrading between the different levels is by way of waist-high glass partitions, framed in oak. The third hexagon is the garage, built of blockwork and clad on the outside in western red cedar.

"The house cost us around £400,000 to build and has showed us little profit so far," says Alan. "But making money on the build was not the point. We have a good joint income and we wanted to create something fantastic to live in. We feel it is worth every penny." ∎

◀ The unusual shapes of the the roof sections meant the design had to be exact from the start. "It was a project with difficult geometry," says architect John Thompson.

Fact File costs as of Aug 2001

NAMES: Alan and Joan Cowell

PROFESSIONS: Headteachers

AREA: South Wales

HOUSE TYPE: Four bedroom green oak frame

HOUSE SIZE: 370m² + store + garage

BUILD ROUTE: Self as main contractor

CONSTRUCTION: Oak frame set into blockwork, with stone and cedar boarding on outer skin

WARRANTY: Architect's certificate

SAP RATING: 88

FINANCE: Private and mortgage from Portman BS

BUILD TIME: Eleven months

LAND COST: £45,000

BUILD COST: £400,000

TOTAL COST: £445,000

CURRENT VALUE: £400,000

COST/M²: £1,081

Cost Breakdown:

Groundworks	£50,000
Oak frame + sandblasting	£63,000
Windows, balustrading, external doors	£110,000
Roof	£22,000
Stone + erection of outer leaf	£25,000
Internal slate and stone features and bathroom marble	£3,000
UFH and plumbing	£12,000
Kitchen	£14,000
Bathrooms	£8,000
Additional labour	£30,000
Construction of link between garage and house	£20,000
Fees	£25,000
Sundries	£18,000
TOTAL	**£400,000**

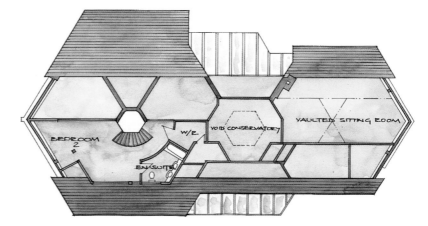

First Floor

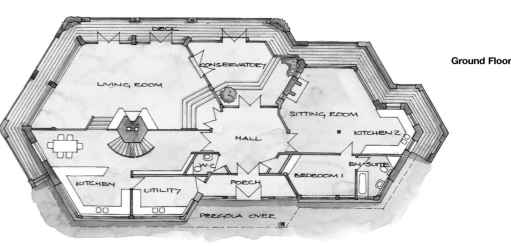

Ground Floor

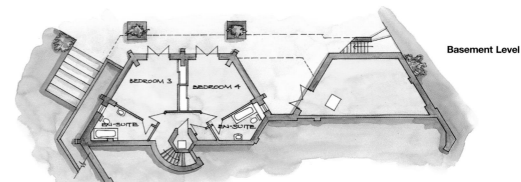

Basement Level

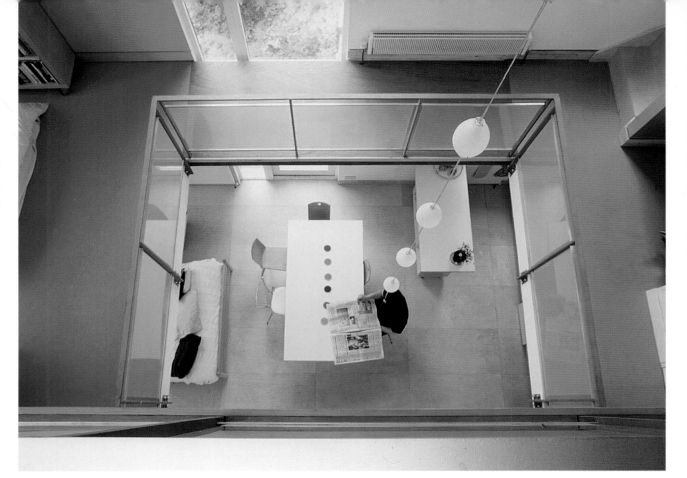

LOW COST HIGH RISE

Architects Alison Davies and Steve Banks have built a remarkable contemporary home above Nottingham jettied out from its hillside site on steel stilts.

"At first, the postman delivered the mail right to the door," says Alison Davies, recalling with a smile the week she and husband Steve Banks moved into their new hillside home, separated from the suburban sprawl of Nottingham below by fifty two steel steps. "Then our post began to be left lower and lower down the stairs each successive day."

Alison and Steve had never imagined the postman would ascend to their front door each day, but back in February '99 when they first moved in, they had no heating, no hot water, no floor finishes and hadn't even thought about the decorating. Installing a postbox to save the postman's knees was not even a priority.

"With our budget and finances stretched to the absolute limit we had to move in at the earliest possible date," recalls Alison, who admits that when they started out on

their self-build odyssey they had little more than ambition and dreams. "This project was the biggest 'wing and a prayer' we could ever have embarked on. We had no equity, no money in the bank and we were still paying rent, so time was of the essence."

"We were definitely a bit naïve when we started out and this was brought to an abrupt end when the contractors' quotes for the building work came back," admits Steve. "Even the lowest quote was way over the £60,000 we had hoped to build for. I was really disheartened at that point. I actually thought of just giving up and selling the plot on with planning permission."

Somehow, perhaps through the strength of a shared dream but probably because the building society agreed to cough up an extra £10,000, vision and determination won through. "We managed to cobble together another ▶

Words: **Michael Holmes**
Photography: **Mark Welsh**

"Local people think its a bit of a peep show but we don't feel that in any way...."

◄ The house sits on a hill overlooking the city of Nottingham (ALSO SEE ABOVE).

£10,000 from various sources," admits Alison, "bringing our total budget up to £80,000. Even with the extra money though, we had to set about a radical rethink of the build contract, the specification and the level of our own involvement.

"We had produced a very detailed works schedule and asked our contractor to provide a fully itemised breakdown of the costings. We discovered that some items were disproportionately expensive so we took these out of the contract and dealt with them ourselves.

"We had to cut a lot of corners to get the house built," admits Alison. "We feel we could have built it for less, had we needed to, because there are still lots of luxuries that we could have cut back on. It's a case of having to cut your cloth to fit, trading off one item for another. Of course, we could equally have spent a great deal more and we do have ideas for around £20,000 more work when funds allow, including a bridge from the top floor out to a landscaped back garden."

In all, Alison and Steve reckon to have taken on about twenty per cent of the building work themselves. They could have chosen to manage the day to day running of the project to reduce costs further but as they both work

The site ▶ originally had planning for three traditional executive homes, but the developer had gone bust in the late 80s. Alison and Steve bought the site, originally marketed at £150,000 for £14,000, splitting it in two with another architect.

◀ At the core of
the house is a
dramatic triple
height space.

full time at their community architecture practice, they concluded that this was simply not a viable option.

"Having a builder also solved out cashflow needs," explains Alison. "We set out a payment schedule in the contract based on completion of set stages in the construction and agreed these with our lender, the Derbyshire Building Society. We simply couldn't have bought materials and paid for subcontractors ourselves."

So short were they of cash that Alison and Steve even bought their plot using an unsecured personal loan.

"In all, Alison and Steve reckon to have taken on about twenty per cent of the work themselves...."

Located in an unfashionable district bordering the affluent and working class suburbs of Nottingham, Steve describes the sporadic development along the dead end street on which they live as "a potted history of English suburban architecture, brought right up to date." Ironically, the only legacy of the consumerist '80s – an era which saw one of ▶

the century's greatest property booms – are the concrete foundations underneath their new house left by a developer driven to bankruptcy by the '89 slump.

Visible for miles around, the three huge grey lumps protruding from the hillside had become the subjects of regular complaints so, despite the radical design, the council were quite relieved at Alison and Steve's development proposal and recommended approval.

"The planners were extremely open minded," says Steve. "However, they wanted us to build them a turning circle at the end of the road in exchange for consent. This would have blown our budget apart and seemed totally unfair." They indicated their willingness to go to appeal over the

issue and this threat proved sufficient to get the planners to back down.

The success of this project hinged on the clever solution to building on the steeply sloping site – a problem that had contributed, in part, to the former owner's demise. Although the original foundations were ten years old, they were still in good condition so Alison and Steve devised a scheme using a lightweight timber frame structure that sits partly on these original foundations, with the front jettied out over the hillside, supported by a steel frame.

The concrete and steel frame, shaped like an H and built into the slab, solved the structural issues, leaving Alison and Steve free to use as much glass and open space within the timber frame as they desired.

"Our previous home was the complete antithesis," says Alison. "A rented two bedroom flat in a Victorian Gothic semi. It was very inward looking, dark and cold, there were no views and no daylight. In a reaction to this compartmentalised environment, we went a bit mad on space. We decided that we'd rather pay for architectural space than rooms."

"Because it's just the two of us, we've chosen a single open plan space in preference to multiple rooms," says Steve. "The design is modern and contemporary, reflecting our priorities as architects. The magnificent views more than compensate for having to stagger up the stairs.

"The stairs do mean that we buy no more than two bags of shopping at once but they are not a big deal. We only have to do it twice a day and it's the only exercise we get. What's more, you never get any door to door salesmen. The only exception was a Jehovah's Witness."

With all that glass and no curtains is the reverse view not an issue? "You can see movement and lights from outside and local people think it is a bit of a peep show,

The first ▼ **storey living area includes a balcony with spectacular views. All of the joinery was made by the Sashless Window Company.**

but we don't feel that in any way," says Steve.

"I felt a bit like a rabbit caught in the headlights at first," admits Alison, "but now I am totally uninhibited. It's really nice and rather liberating in a way. You get used to anything."

"Absolutely gobsmacked," was how Alison and Steve describe their reaction to winning the Daily Telegraph Homebuilding & Renovating Awards '99. "This project has absolutely changed things," says Steve, seemingly unsure whether it is entirely for the good. "We have made various choices in life that have not been financially rewarding…" "but suddenly we are a bankable proposition," interjects Alison who seems more at ease with their success. "In contrast to our work, most of which is for voluntary groups and charities, the house was entirely selfishly driven — we've found success and made money by mistake!"

"It's all fallen into place quite nicely but it didn't happen by accident," interrupts Steve. "We took a risk…" Alison agrees, "and we are now, amazingly, sitting on an asset that will make lots of things possible. It was far, far more that we bargained for when we initially entered the Awards." ∎

The master bedroom includes a roof terrace, which is yet to be completed, with wooden decking and glass infill panel in the railing.

Fact File

NAMES: Alison Davies & Steve Banks	
PROFESSIONS: Architects	
AREA: Carlton, Nottingham	
HOUSE TYPE: Three storey detached	
HOUSE SIZE: 116m²	
BUILD ROUTE: Main contractor plus 20% DIY	
CONSTRUCTION: Timber frame on	steel

SAP RATING: 82		
FINANCE: Derbyshire BS		
BUILD TIME: Five months		
LAND COST: £7,000		
BUILD COST: £80,000	**13%**	
TOTAL COST: £87,000	**COST SAVING**	
HOUSE VALUE: £100,000		
COST/m²: £690		

USEFUL CONTACTS: Architect - Groundworks: 0115 941 7007; Structural Engineer - Price and Myers: 0115 950 7977; Contractor - Robert Woodhead Ltd: 01623 871515; Frame - Midland Timber Engineering: 01530 230262; Joinery - The Sashless Window Co: 01609 780202

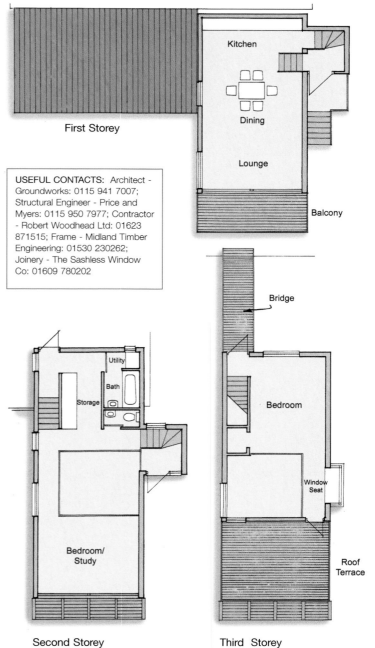

Laura Fennell and Alison Richards have built a modern ranch-style home designed to make the most of views over the surrounding countryside.

Words:
Clive Fewins

Photography:
Justin Paul

When Laura Fennell and Alison Richards found the third of an acre plot of land beside a bend in the Grand Union Canal, eight miles from Aylesbury, Bucks, they could hardly believe their luck. It was the first building plot they had looked at, having spent several fruitless months searching for a large house of any age providing it had character and appealed to them.

"Our aim was to pool our resources and combine our two small houses into one larger, preferably four bedroom home," says Laura. "When, by chance, we asked one of the agents we were dealing with about plots, he said this one was about to come onto the market. We immediately looked at it and realised it was a wonderful site that would be ideal if we were prepared to become self-builders. It was only later when we read the self-build magazines and attended exhibitions that we learned of the problems other self-builders were experiencing finding a site and realised how extremely fortunate we were."

At first they were rather apprehensive about self-building, but they were spurred on by the thought that Laura's brother-in-law, Colin Luscombe, who had recently had to give up his bricklaying job due to a serious injury, would be available to help them supervise the job when neither of them were around. For most of the time, however, they undertook the supervision themselves, as well as undertaking all the project management. Laura had already given up her job and was a full-time student doing a science degree 40 miles away at Royal Holloway College. Alison continued to work in her London-based high technology sales job.

The site, which they bought for £127,000, came with detailed planning permission for a four-bedroomed house. This was also a stroke of luck, because although Laura and ▶

The distinctive ▶ cedar cladding has weathered well, taking on a silver colour two years after being installed.

Southern Comfort

Building a contemporary ranch style home

"By doing a self-build we have managed to skip two or three steps on our way up the housing ladder…"

A spacious ▲ open plan living space takes up the entire first floor.

Alison wanted to print their own stamp on the house that was eventually built, they gained a lot of ideas from the house that was planned, not least the external timber cladding and the 'upside down' concept that they have opted for, with the main living space upstairs and the bedrooms beneath.

Local architects Hinton Cook, whom they commissioned shortly after buying the plot in February 1998, went along with this scheme, coming up with the idea of a top-lit brick-faced curved stair tower at the front of the building with a front balcony accessed from the upstairs. This was aimed at providing some relief at the front of the straightforward pitched roofed building.

"We love the staircase. It imports light from the top and front," says Laura. "As the front faces approximately north we have placed fewer windows on that side as it is the rear that looks over the canal and has all the views. The noise factor was also a consideration, as a main railway line runs along the other side of the road."

At the other ▶ end of the first floor open plan room lies the kitchen (Magnet 01535 661133) and informal dining area.

"One of the main things that we like about the house is the way that this one big first floor room runs the full 14 metre length of the house," says Alison. "It is wonderful to get back to in the evening – so light and spacious. It has really enhanced our lives and is so different from the small compartmentalised homes we lived in previously."

▶

Apart from the first floor verandah and the curved stair tower with its splendidly solid beech staircase, there are several other interesting pieces of design. They include the doorless 'wet room', based on a Dutch model, that serves as the en suite bathroom attached to the master bedroom downstairs; also the wood strip floors which run throughout and, of course, the exterior horizontal cedar cladding.

"We adore living here and there are very few things we would do differently…"

"Choosing the cladding timber was a big decision," says Laura. "We could have opted for the much cheaper Baltic Pine or Douglas Fir, but we chose cedar because of ease of maintenance and longevity. We think we chose correctly because after two-and-a-half years it has matured to a beautiful silver colour. Fortunately we were in the position of being able to buy high quality fittings when we felt it appropriate. Apart from this our only real 'luxuries' were the internal doors and the second floor that we fitted upstairs. The main reason for a second floor on top of the one supplied by the timber frame company was to accommodate the underfloor heating which we had decided to extend to the first floor, as we had very little wall space for radiators. We feel it also adds that bit of extra insulation between the floors."

Fitting the additional floor plus all the underfloor heating loops at first floor level was one of the many tasks Laura and Alison undertook themselves. Together with friends they also laid the beam and block ground floor, including doing the all the cutting needed at the base of the curved stairwell. After moving in during November

1999 they spent two more years carrying out all the internal finishing work. This included all the decorating, most of the tiling, fitting doorframes, architraves and skirting and other carpentry, and also cladding the outside of the double garage with cedar.

The build proved relatively straightforward, although they regret that in order not to overdevelop the plot their planning authority, Aylesbury Vale, made them 'squeeze' the house in length, slightly reducing the sizes of the two spare bedrooms downstairs.

"Most of the subcontractors, apart from one 'carpenter from hell' were fine and we had few difficulties apart from the usual problems of co-ordinating the different subcontractors," says Laura. "We had a problem with the roof trusses. We had made it quite plain to Taylor Lane, who manufactured and supplied the timber frame, that these were to form a feature in the roof, but when they arrived they were full of knots and gaps. When we complained a director of the company visited us and agreed to clad them in Douglas Fir at no extra cost to ourselves. We think they now look fine.

"We found it extremely hard to find good carpenters and plumbers and the build overran, largely because it took 16 weeks to get planning consent rather than the eight weeks we had anticipated. However, we believe the project has been a good use of our time and that by doing a self-build we have gone up two or three steps in the housing ladder. Now it is finished and I have gained my degree I am looking for another job."

Alison says: "We adore living here and there are very few things we would do differently with the benefit of hindsight. Perhaps we should have planned a log-burning stove into the upper floor. We might still fit one, although it could make it too hot. Certainly we could have managed with fewer sliding doors on the first floor. Despite having double-glazed argon-filled panes we have still found them draughty in winter.

"But basically it has worked. As women we were naturally apprehensive to begin with, but we had excellent support from family and friends. It was a relatively short period of stress for something that we find a great joy to live in. Although we had no absolute budget we were careful throughout to make sure we were not spending more on the build than the house would be worth. We need have had no fears." ■

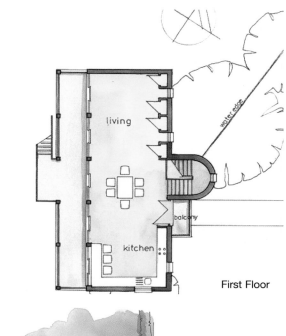

First Floor

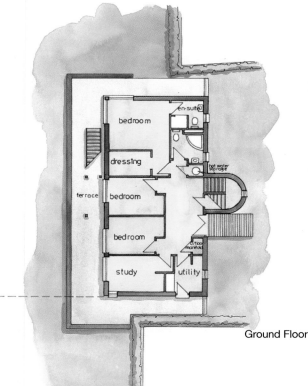

Ground Floor

Fact File costs as of June 2002

NAMES: Laura Fennell & Alison Richards

PROFESSIONS: Sales executive and unemployed

AREA: Buckinghamshire

HOUSE TYPE: Four bedroomed contemporary style with bedrooms on ground floor and open plan room on first floor

HOUSE SIZE: 200m²

BUILD ROUTE: Selves as main contractors

CONSTRUCTION: Timber frame

WARRANTY: Zurich building guarantee

SAP RATING: 95

FINANCE: Sales of two houses plus £150,000 Bradford and Bingley self-build mortgage.

BUILD TIME: Twelve months

LAND COST: £127,000

BUILD COST: £147,500

TOTAL COST: £274,500

HOUSE VALUE: £410,000

COST/m²: £737

33% COST SAVING

Cost Breakdown

Groundworks:	£11,000
Services and septic tank:	£3,800
Fees:	£4,600
Finance costs	£2,000
Piled foundations:	£15,000
Beam and block ground floor	£1,800
Timber frame:	£23,600
Roof:	£5,500
Windows:	£16,000
Doors and associated joinery:	£4,700
Timber cladding:	£8,000
Brick cladding:	£2,000
Heating:	£3,500
Bathrooms:	£3,200
Kitchen:	£5,900
Scaffolding and equipment hire:	£3,600
Internal flooring:	£2,200
Staircase:	£2,700
Deck and balcony:	£4,400
Plumbing:	£4,500
Electrician:	£4,200
Plastering and screeding:	£6,800
Decoration:	£500
Miscellaneous:	£8,000
TOTAL	**£147,500**

USEFUL CONTACTS: **Architect** - Hinton Cook: 01296 662189; **Piling** - Mini-Piling: 01527 529555; **Groundworks** - Puttnams: 01844 347944; **Timber frame** - Taylor Lane: 01432 271912; **Beam and block ground floor** - RMC: 0117 937 3740; **Plumber** - P J Willis: 01296 688229; **Electrics** - FJB: 01296 482683; **Roofer** - Ted Butler: 01494 785195; **Stairs** - Andy Steggall: 01844 237708; **Underfloor heating** - David Robbens: 0800 45 45 69; **Balustrading** - Davroy: 01525 714823; **Windows** - Sunfold: 01362 699744; **Internal doors** - The Real Door Co: 01462 451230; **Timber floor** - Mainline: 01403 738222; **Fibre slate roofing** - Sandtoft: 01427 872696; **Sanitaryware** - Grant and Stone: 01296 393959

California Dreaming

Creating a contemporary
West Coast style home in Dorset

Words:
Debbie Jeffery

Photography:
Nigel Rigden

**Alan Wood
wanted a modern
house, suitable
for entertaining
large numbers of
people, with
generous
expanses of glass
to provide a light
and spacious feel.**

Alan Wood has built a light and
spacious contemporary style home
designed around a central atrium living
space and featuring an indoor pool.

"I built this house in reaction to Poundbury," smiles Alan
Wood. His spacious, contemporary new home in Dorset
could not be further removed from the traditional urban
design of the local development championed by the Prince
of Wales. The architecture at Poundbury draws on the rich
heritage of Dorset and, in particular, the attractive streets
of Dorchester, using local and often recycled materials.

Although he does not deny the quality of materials and
attention to detail of the village, Alan Wood's ideas are
slightly more forward thinking. "Don't misunderstand me
– I do appreciate why people like old houses," he explains.
"I wanted to build something which was of our time,
however, and to incorporate up-to-the-minute innovations
and technologies. A totally contemporary house, without
compromise. I'm not a revisionist – I want to move
forward – but it proved impossible to buy a large modern
house in this area."

Inspired by his travels to the Far East, Alan – the
Director of Buying for New Look, and a leading figure in
the retail fashion sector – has stayed in more hotels than
he cares to remember. "Places like Thailand and Japan
have had a lasting effect on me," he says. "There's quite a
minimalist approach to their philosophy for life. Many of
my ideas for the house came from modern hotels, which
have impressive atriums and lots of natural light. Coming
from a country that can be grey and miserable, and being
a person who craves daylight, I just wanted to live in that
kind of environment."

▶

A Portland stone wall in the grounds
continues through the centre of the
house itself – anchoring it to the plot.

"Brockwood has outstripped even my dreams, and has changed the way I live…"

The central ▲ two storey atrium is enclosed by a first floor gallery providing access between the four corner towers and lit by an impressive roof lantern. A helical staircase sweeps up from this space to the first floor accommodation (SEE NEXT PAGE).

Set in four acres and surrounded by woodland, his site is sheltered from its neighbours but benefits from being within walking distance of the village pub. Previously owned by one of Alan's friends, the plot was overgrown and occupied by a small cottage which had been extended in the 1960s and 70s. "To do anything with the existing house would have proved very expensive and restrictive," Alan explains. "I knew that I wanted to build something more fitting for such a unique site."

After trawling through hundreds of books, magazines and web sites in search of buildings to inspire him, he approached architects Cheshire Robbins Design. An innovative house designed by the practice on a difficult site had caught his eye and, by pure coincidence, he discovered that they were also based in Dorset.

The result is Brookwood: a 658m² house with an internal swimming pool and detached lodge suitable for staff or visitors. Large areas of glass provide a light and spacious feel, whilst private spaces are secured within solid corners around an open plan core used primarily for living and entertaining.

The design was supported by the local planning department, but considered too modern for its conservation area setting by local councillors, and refused. A subsequent appeal was upheld, however, with the inspector stating: "It is certainly an unequivocally modern design, aiming to be an unashamed product of its own time — as are several of the principal houses in the area. I consider that the scheme is an exciting example of modern architecture, with the potential to enhance the conservation area by contributing to the continuing evolution of its architectural heritage."

A contract sum was negotiated with Poole-based contractor Edward Jackson, whose experience of civil engineering was considered to be beneficial to the type of construction required. "I explained to the architect that I wanted someone to build the house who would really put their heart into it," says Alan. The contractor, who had previously worked with Cheshire Robbins, was employed using a JCT Intermediate Form of contract, and work started on site in September 2000.

▶

"I really have to pinch myself and think how lucky I am to own such a fantastic new home."

Enabling work included demolition of the existing dwelling, new fencing to the perimeter and de-watering to allow the construction of the swimming pool. The project was due for completion by mid-summer 2001 but overran until November due to excessively wet weather conditions: it rained almost non-stop for six months. Even so, everyone involved in the project remained on extremely good terms, and the standard of workmanship proved consistently high.

Foundations were short bored piles with in-situ ground beams, due to the high water table. The basic structural composition is load bearing stone and blockwork to the corner towers, with steel supports to the central atrium area. Beam and block flooring was specified for the corners of the first floor, with a timber 'silent floor' to the gallery.

Anti-cracking, white insulated render is the predominant external facing material, with feature stone walls providing a contrast. All doors, windows and rooflights are colour coated aluminium frames, with double glazed 'K' glass, and the main roof is finished with a 3-coat torch-on integrated waterproofing and insulation system, concealed beneath a parapet upstand.

Working in the fashion industry ensures that Alan Wood has his finger firmly on the pulse. Low voltage lighting was specified throughout Brookwood, with a central unit controlling different lighting moods, along with integrated audio and video facilities, plus fire and security protection.

"Like most people, I have worked my way up the property ladder — starting off in a modern flat, followed by ▶

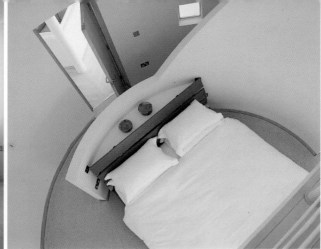

The white kitchen and utility room units, as well as the kitchen in the lodge, were all fitted out for £25,000 including appliances and contrasting dark marble worktops. From K&B: 01722 334800

a new house in a village setting and then moving to a property situated on a cliff in Weymouth," says Alan. "Brookwood has outstripped even my dreams, however, and has changed the way I live. I am now far more home based, and more active due to the swimming pool and workout area.

"Before, I tended to spend much of my time entertaining in restaurants — but now I can accommodate large numbers of friends at home, and I also have a working office here." Each bedroom has its own en suite bathroom, with friends debating who will stay in the 'round room', with its raised bathroom overlooking the bed (ABOVE RIGHT).

Despite its size Brookwood is not an overpowering building, and Alan is comfortable spending time there on his own. None of the living spaces exist in isolation, and there are no connecting passageways or corridors.

"The virtual tour of the house which Cheshire Robbins showed me before it was built made me feel as if I had been here before," he remarks. "One thing I had never experienced, however, is waking up, going for a swim and having a feeling of sheer joy at living in the house. I really have to pinch myself and think how lucky I am to own such a fantastic new home." ∎

Fact File costs as of March 2003

NAME: Alan Wood

PROFESSION: Buying Director

AREA: Dorset

HOUSE TYPE: Four bedroom detached plus one bedroom lodge

HOUSE SIZE: 658m²

BUILD ROUTE: Building contractor

CONSTRUCTION: Rendered blockwork and stone

WARRANTY: NHBC Buildmark

SAP RATING: 94

FINANCE: HSBC

BUILD TIME: 15 months

LAND COST: £300,000

BUILD COST: £660,000

TOTAL COST: £960,000

HOUSE VALUE: £1.5m

COST/m²: £1,003

36% COST SAVING

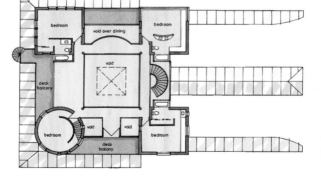

Large, formal living areas are centrally positioned to the ground floor. Four first floor corner bedrooms are set around a gallery overlooking the central atrium, which draws natural light into the heart of the house.

Ground Floor

First Floor

USEFUL CONTACTS: **Architect** - Cheshire Robbins Design Limited: 01202 473344; **Main contractor** - Edward Jackson Ltd: 07774 940240; **Structural Engineer** - Oscar Faber: 0117 9017000; Environs Partnership: 01305 250455; **Helical stairs** - Crescent of Cambridge Ltd: 01480 301522; **Windows** - Pennington Lacey & Sons: 02380 631555; **Flooring** – Peter Newman Flooring Ltd: 01202 747175; **Swimming pool** - Cresta Leisure Ltd: 01305 834969; **Fixings** - Allfix Distributors: 01202 519066; **Plumbing** - Colin J Brumble Ltd: 01305 766549; **Demolition** - Bermacross Ltd: 01258 473309; **Builders & Timber Merchants** - Jewsons Ltd: 01305 786611; Eagle (Wessex) Plant Ltd: 01305 775656; Roger Bullivant Piling Ltd: 01373 865012; **External render** - Marmorit (UK): 0117 9821042; **Special roof timbers** - Crendon Timber Ltd: 01305 847110 Cumberland Reinforcement Ltd: 01202 743311; **Portland stone** - Easton Masonry (UK) Ltd: 01305 861020; **Roofing** – Gorvin Roofing: 01202 676443; **Bricklaying** - R G Horlock: 01305 834134; **Groundworks** - T J Kelly: 01202 874129; **Painter** - T J Spears: 01305 787586; Hanson Concrete & Aggregates: 01373 463211; **Electrics** - D Johnson: 01202 873257; **Carpentry** - R R Hobby: 01202 731420; **Plastering** - D J Taylor: 01202 733332; **Spiral stairs and railings** - Mowlam Metalcraft: 01305 250655; Weymouth Scaffolding: 01305 783021

LOOKING FOR A BUILDING PLOT?

www.plotfinder.net
ONLINE LAND AND RENOVATION DATABASE

www.plotfinder.net is an online database which holds details of **over 5,700** building plots and properties in need of renovation or conversion currently for sale in the UK.

Save time - endless effort and time can be spent trawling through papers, calling estate agents and going to auctions, **let www.plotfinder.net do it for you.**

A dedicated team are in touch with a network of over 11,000 contacts to source **building land**, **renovations** and **conversions**. Every lising on the website is checked for availability regularly so you don't waste time following up sold plots or properties.

LOOKING FOR A RENOVATION PROJECT?

LOOKING FOR A PROPERTY TO CONVERT?

BENEFITS OF
www.plotfinder.net

■ FREE email alert when new plots are added to your chosen counties.

■ Unlimited access to the www.plotfinder.net database for any five counties.

■ Save favourite plots into a separate folder.

■ Mark viewed plots as read.

■ The website gives you instant access to the database (updated daily).

Visit www.plotfinder.net to Subscribe
One year subscription ONLY £40!

Price correct at time of going to press, to check current prices please visit www.plotfinder.net

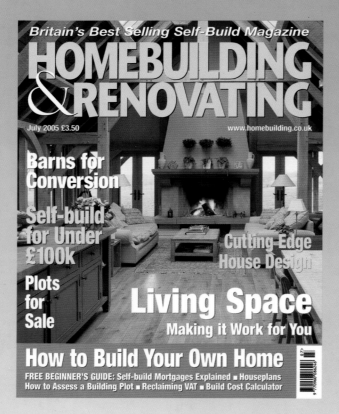

COVER PHOTOGRAPHY: NIGEL RIGDEN

BACK COVER PHOTOGRAPHY: PHILIP BIER, VIEW PICTURES (LEFT),

NIGEL RIGDEN (TOP) & JEREMY PHILLIPS (RIGHT)

PUBLISHED BY ASCENT PUBLISHING LIMITED

2 SUGAR BROOK COURT

ASTON ROAD, BROMSGROVE

WORCESTERSHIRE

B60 3EX

© 2005 ASCENT PUBLISHING LIMITED

ALL RIGHTS RESERVED

ISBN 0-9544669-9-3

PRINTED IN CHINA THROUGH PHOENIX OFFSET

A **HOMEBUILDING & RENOVATING** BOOK

www.homebuilding.co.uk

homebuilding@centaur.co.uk

HOMEBUILDING
&RENOVATING
M A G A Z I N E

CONTEMPORARY HOMES

19 INSPIRATIONAL INDIVIDUALLY DESIGNED HOMES

Ascent Publishing Limited
A CENTAUR HOLDINGS PLC COMPANY

Sugar Brook Court, Aston Road,
Bromsgrove, Worcestershire, B60 3EX
Tel: 01527 834400 Fax: 01527 834497
E-mail: homebuilding@centaur.co.uk